For the Potential Christian

For the Potential Christian

— Basic Answers to Basic Questions —

Miranda L. Turner

RESOURCE *Publications* • Eugene, Oregon

FOR THE POTENTIAL CHRISTIAN
Basic Answers to Basic Questions

Copyright © 2021 Miranda L. Turner. All rights reserved. Except for brief quotations in critical publications or reviews, no part of this book may be reproduced in any manner without prior written permission from the publisher. Write: Permissions, Wipf and Stock Publishers, 199 W. 8th Ave., Suite 3, Eugene, OR 97401.

Resource Publications
An Imprint of Wipf and Stock Publishers
199 W. 8th Ave., Suite 3
Eugene, OR 97401

www.wipfandstock.com

PAPERBACK ISBN: 978-1-5326-9054-9
HARDCOVER ISBN: 978-1-5326-9055-6
EBOOK ISBN: 978-1-5326-9056-3

01/20/21

Bible translations used are as follows:

Holy Bible, New International Version® (NIV®), copyright ©1973, 1978, 1984, 2011 by Biblica, Inc.™ Used by permission. All rights reserved worldwide.

New King James Version® (NKJV), copyright © 1982 by Thomas Nelson. Used by permission. All rights reserved.

Holy Bible, English Standard Version® (ESV®), copyright © 2001 by Crossway, a publishing ministry of Good News Publishers. All rights reserved. ESV Text Edition: 2016.

Holy Bible, New Living Translation (NLT), copyright © 1996, 2004, 2007, 2013, 2015 by Tyndale House Foundation. Used by permission of Tyndale House Publishers Inc., Carol Stream, Illinois 60188. All rights reserved.

In loving memory of my mother,
Jacquelyn Smith-Turner,
13 April 1956—17 June 2017.

Because she let Jesus change her life,
I saw there was hope that he could change mine too.

For God so loved the world that he gave his one and only Son, that whoever believes in him shall not perish but have eternal life.

—JOHN 3:16 NIV

Contents

Acknowledgements | ix
Introduction | xi

Chapter 1: Why Christianity? | 1
Chapter 2: A Side Note | 7
Chapter 3: What Is Faith? | 14
Chapter 4: The One True God | 21
Chapter 5: What Is Sin? | 33
Chapter 6: Jesus: The Lamb of God | 41
Chapter 7: Satan: The Enemy of Our Souls | 50
Chapter 8: Hell: Punishment for the Wicked | 55
Chapter 9: Heaven: The Reward of the Righteous | 60
Chapter 10: What Does It Mean to Repent? | 65
Chapter 11: What Is Salvation? | 73
Chapter 12: Would You Like to Accept Jesus? | 80
Chapter 13: So, What Now? | 84

Bibliography | 93

Acknowledgements

THANK YOU, LORD JESUS Christ, for giving me this opportunity and for using me for this project. It is in you that I live, move, and have my being and I could do nothing apart from you. You've walked me through this entire process and you've amazed me at every corner. If it weren't for your strength, wisdom, and encouragement, this book would have never been completed. All glory goes to you. I love you with all that is in me.

Thank you, Mama, for exposing me to God at a young age by sending me to church even though I didn't want to go. Little did I know it would be the beginning of the most beautiful and most important relationship I would ever have. I believe you would be proud of me if you were here to see all God is doing in my life now. He has been more than faithful. I love you. Rest in peace. I can hardly wait to see you again.

Thank you to all the wise pastors, evangelists, Christian leaders, and men and women of God, both past and present, who share the godly wisdom they receive with the world. It has allowed me to gain a better understanding about the things of God and has taught me how to walk upright and pleasing in his sight. I appreciate the fact that you don't compromise God's Word and I commend you for standing up for truth. You are a great example and inspiration to me.

To anyone who has encouraged me to do anything of value, anyone who has spoken a kind or edifying word, and everyone who believed in me to go further than where the world told me

Acknowledgements

I could go—thank you. I truly believe all things are possible with God, and that this is only the beginning. May God continue to bless you all.

Introduction

As a little girl, my mother would send me, my two older sisters, and my older brother to church nearly every Sunday. We weren't true followers of Jesus Christ but we had a certain level of respect for the Lord. In other words, we held a general belief in God and acknowledged he was the creator of the world, but we rejected the godly lifestyle. We were what some people would call "Sunday Christians," meaning we would play the part by dressing up and attending church the first day of the week, but on the other days we were unmistakably Satan's offspring.

I can't tell you the number of times I sat in the back pew and heard the pastor speak the Word of God, yet walked away with nothing to show for it. I heard the words but I didn't know what they meant. Of course, being distracted by an intense game of tic-tac-toe didn't help either. We didn't have cell phones back then—only pen and paper—so we used what we had to pass the time.

I didn't appreciate religion. I didn't understand the whole church thing or what the true purpose of it was. I just thought it was a place we had to go if we didn't want to go to hell. And boy, was I afraid to go to hell. That's what initially prompted me to begin praying. Sometimes, when I was alone, I would pray and ask God to save me. I didn't want anyone to find out because I thought they'd think it was foolish. Who? *Me?* One of those church folks? Get real. So I never spoke to anyone about it except God.

But here's the funny thing. I had no idea how to pray, nor did I even know what it meant to be saved. However, in true

Introduction

ignorance, I continued to pray the best way I knew how, with a sincere heart. After praying, I would try my best to "live right." I would promise to stop doing this and to start doing that, but it never lasted for more than a few hours. After being disappointed at my failure, I would shake off my foolishness for thinking God would save somebody like me, and I'd run back to the arms of the devil, who gladly awaited my return. I repeated this same song and dance many times.

Then, as I got older, I stopped going to church and moved further away from God. In my late teens and early twenties, the few godly principles I held began to dwindle down to nothing. I got caught up in the cares of this life and the lusts of this world. But the amazing thing is, now and then I would still feel the Lord tugging at my heart—like a fisherman reeling in a stubborn old fish that won't give in.

I would still pray. Although, now my prayers were more desperate because I'd discovered I had no purpose. Life itself had no meaning to me. Everything I did seemed to only satisfy me for the moment, and once that moment passed I would return to a joyless, unfulfilled life. I was only existing; I wasn't really living. I felt bad about who I'd become, but I was helpless to do anything about it. I was so empty, alone, and depressed.

I would often think to myself, "Now, surely, there has to be more to life than this." I tried God several more times over the years. I would pray, I would try to change, and then I would fail—again. It was like a bad record on repeat. Eventually, I washed my hands of it and gave up hope. But there's one thing we come to learn as we get to know the Lord, and that's that he doesn't give up on us as easily as we give up on ourselves.

I don't know where you are in your spiritual journey, or what it is that's fueling your search for God. Perhaps you're currently where I once was. Maybe you feel there's more to life than what you have and you're looking to find what's missing. Or, maybe you're on a desperate quest to find purpose but you keep coming up empty. You might be going through the greatest difficulty of your life, and you're looking for divine intervention.

Introduction

Has the doctor given you bad news about your health? Is your family falling apart and you're struggling to keep it together? Have you recently lost a loved one and you're in need of comfort and peace? Answers? Are you in desperate need of encouragement before you completely give up and break down?

Whatever your reason, this one thing is certain: If you're looking for *hope*, then you're in the right place. Hope is found in a life surrendered to Jesus Christ. There's hope for the present and hope for the future, in the good times as well as the bad. It's a hope that helps us get through each day no matter our circumstances. So, how does one obtain this hope? Well, it all begins with truth. That is my goal—to make sure you know the truth. Not truth as the world gives it, but the truth that can set you free—freedom from guilt, shame, addiction, and fear.

So if you're curious about Christianity, if you're interested in knowing more about salvation, if you're searching for that new life in Christ you've seen others living, or just looking for rest for your weary soul, then this is all for you. Inside, you will discover basic answers to basic questions such as, "Who is God?," "Who is Jesus?," and "What is salvation?" I've included pieces of my testimony to encourage you, useful tips to guide you, and relevant scriptures to inform you. It is my prayer that you will continue with me through the pages of this book, and as you do, I pray you will be encouraged, enlightened, and blessed. God bless you.

> You will seek me and find me when you seek me with all your heart.[1]

---

1. Jer 29:13 NIV.

— CHAPTER 1 —

Why Christianity?

YOU MAY ASK, "WELL, why Christianity? Why should I believe in the Christian faith over all other beliefs?" It's a valid question indeed, and one that's been asked by many, including myself at one time or another. That's why I regret to inform you that I don't have the answer for you. I believe you must seek and find that answer for yourself.

But, here's the dilemma. With the many religious views and the different doctrines available, how can we truly discover what is true and what is false? How can we possibly place one belief above all the others? We can learn a wealth of information from books and from the testimonies of others, but there's a certain type of knowledge that can only be acquired through experience. Therefore, we must each have our own personal encounter with the one true God.

Truthfully, the only solid evidence I have that proves to me that Christianity is the real deal is my personal experience with Jesus and the changes he's made in my life. No one else can take credit for the chains he's broken, which I couldn't begin to loosen on my own, and no one else could give me the joy I've received since I've come to know him.

Not one soul could successfully argue with what I have personally experienced—not with opinion, or with speculation. I've seen what I've seen, I've felt what I've felt, and I attest that I was in my right mind when it happened. But as with anything else, some will try to explain it away, and some have already tried. Nevertheless, I know what I know and I stand firm on it. That's what I'm praying you'll find as well. Not just information, not just an understanding, but your own unique experience with the one true God—an experience that only comes through faith.

> Oh, taste and see that the Lord is good; Blessed is the man who trusts in Him![1]

What's in It for Me?

The million-dollar question people often ask is, "What's in it for me? How will becoming a Christian benefit my life?" Well, let me begin by telling you a story. Once, there were three Hebrew men named Hananiah, Mishael, and Azariah, better known as Shadrach, Meshach, and Abednego. These young men worshiped and served the Lord with their whole hearts. One day, against their will, they were carried from their home and taken into a foreign land called Babylon. However, because of God's favor, they were placed over the affairs of that province, where they faithfully served the king.

Then, it happened that the king of Babylon, Nebuchadnezzar, made a large image of gold that he set up in the province. He sent for all the leaders to come and attend the dedication of the image. When they were all gathered together at the ceremony, they were told that whenever they heard the sound of certain instruments with all kinds of music, everyone should fall down and worship the golden image.

Whoever did not obey the king's command would be immediately cast into a burning furnace. So, it was done accordingly. When the people heard the music, everyone fell down and worshiped the golden image. That is, everyone except the three Hebrew men. They refused to bow as they would only worship the one true God, Yahweh. They literally took a stand and stood up for what

---

1. Ps 34:8 NKJV.

they believed, which was both brave and noble. But, of course, there will always be someone who fails to mind their own business.

Certain men went and told the king that the Jews he set over the affairs of Babylon had disregarded his command. They advised him that the men didn't serve his gods, nor did they worship the golden image he set up. This made Nebuchadnezzar furious and he commanded that Shadrach, Meshach, and Abednego be brought before him. He asked them if the accusations were true, then he gave them another chance to make it right. He told them that when they hear the sound of the musical instruments and all kinds of music, if they fall down and worship the image then everything will be fine. If they do not worship the image, however, they will be cast into a burning fiery furnace. Wow! Talk about a dilemma. Nevertheless, the young men already had their minds made up.

They told the king that they believed God would save them, but even if he didn't, they would not serve his gods, nor would they worship the golden image he set up. The king became so angry that he ordered the furnace to be heated seven times the normal temperature, then the men were bound up with all their clothing, hats, and other garments, and thrown into the fiery furnace. The furnace was so hot that the flames killed the mighty men who threw them inside. There was nowhere to run and no place to escape. It seemed like the end of the road for these devout men of God.

But suddenly, Nebuchadnezzar rose up. In amazement, he asked his counselors, "Weren't there three men that we tied up and threw into the fire?"[2] "Yes," they replied. "Look!" he answered, "I see four men loose, walking in the midst of the fire; and they are not hurt, and the form of the fourth is like the Son of God."[3] Nebuchadnezzar saw a fourth man in the furnace. It was the Lord! He was with the men in the fire, shielding and protecting them from the flames. King Nebuchadnezzar called the three men to come out of the furnace, and when they did, they were not burned, the hair of their head was not singed, and they didn't

---

2. Dan 3:24 NIV.
3. Dan 3:25 NKJV.

even smell like fire! Afterward, the king not only praised God, but he promoted the trio.

You see, as Christians, we don't get a pass to skate by on a life of ease. We are not exempt from going through the fire, aka, the troubles and trials of this life. However, when we do, we don't go into the furnace alone. Jesus goes in with us. He protects us so we're not utterly consumed by the flames of our circumstances, and he strengthens and encourages us. We still go through life with its ups and downs, but we have an advantage because we know Christ. And because we know how faithful he is, we don't wallow in sorrow or despair, but we turn to him in times of trouble, and he helps us. Jesus is our firefighter!

Another advantage of living for the Lord is the fact that Christians experience the fullness of God's love and the fulfillment of his promises. There's no mistake about it. God is good. He showers his kindness on both believers and unbelievers alike. However, just as we love all children but treat our own the best, certain promises God reserves specifically for his children—the true followers of Jesus Christ.

As Christians, we can lay aside fear because we trust in our God. We don't have to worry about tomorrow's problems because we know he's in control of tomorrow. He promises all our needs will be supplied, and in difficult trials he promises peace that is beyond our ability to understand it. Instead of temporary happiness, which the world provides, he gives us pure and lasting joy. He will bless the work of our hands, give us victory over our enemies, and everything we do will prosper. Unfortunately, there are too many promises to list here, but I encourage you to open the Bible and discover the numerous blessings that will be available to you as a child of God.

Now, these are all great benefits, however, they're only perks that come along with serving the Lord. The ultimate reward for living faithful to Christ is eternal life. We no longer live with fear of death, since we know when we leave this world, our home awaits in heaven. We understand this life and the things in it are temporary, and we are mere strangers passing through. Therefore, no matter what goes on in the world—whether sickness, disease, famine, etc.—our eyes remain fixed on our eternal abode. This is why we hope in Jesus.

What Does It Mean to Be a Christian?

What comes to mind when you think of a Christian? Have you considered what it really means to be a follower of Jesus Christ? Regardless of what you might have seen or heard, Christians are not some happy-go-lucky churchgoing weirdos. We are human beings with real issues. The only difference between Christians and non-Christians is the fact that Christians have decided our method of living wasn't working. Therefore, we've forsaken our own way to follow the One who knows the beginning and the end of all things—the One who has all the answers who loves and cares for us deeply—the One who is the man Jesus Christ.

His love has compelled us to put away our immoral standards, to strive to live up to his moral perfection. Although we are none perfect naturally, we aim to be spiritually perfect and pleasing in his sight. We fall short every day, but his grace makes up for what we lack when we miss the target of his perfection. There are no "super-saints" who have "arrived" at the peak of holiness. Rather, God's Spirit constantly shapes and molds us to reflect the character of Christ, and our transformation is a continuous journey—one with a destination at which we will not arrive until the day we open our eyes in heaven.

I feel that last point is important because many people are intimidated by Christianity, or discouraged because they feel they can't live up to its expectations. But salvation is not for people who have it all together. On the contrary, it's for those who are broken. It's for those who've realized they can't make it through this life on their own, and that if they're going to pull through, it's not going to be by their own strength.

So, if you've been hesitant to give your life to Christ for this reason, don't be so hard on yourself. If you can simply believe and have faith, then you have what it takes to become a Christian, thus

For the Potential Christian

receiving the joy of the Lord and securing your place in heaven. So, who can be saved? Who can have eternal life? Who is the potential Christian? The one who is willing to believe.

> But as many as received Him, to them He gave the right to become children of God, to those who believe in His name.[4]

---

4. John 1:12 NKJV.

— Chapter 2 —

A Side Note

Before we continue, I would like you to do me a favor. Right now, I want you to throw out your preconceptions about Christianity, set aside human reasoning, and suppress that little voice that tends to rise up and challenge anything outside of the norm. Why? Because when it comes to the things of God, our thoughts and our human understanding are limited, yet we tend to try and explain everything.

When we can't make sense of something, we're quick to toss it out like the container of food that's been hiding in the back of the fridge for weeks; it's just too much of a mystery. So, although useful in many situations, our excellent reasoning skills can be a hindrance to our faith if we try to reason from our own viewpoint. We must begin with God's Word and then build on that foundation.

However, I will suggest something that might help you. It might help if you go ahead and accept the fact that there are some things you and I just aren't going to understand. That's because no one understands them. But that's true for any religion or belief and not just Christianity, so I don't think my suggestion to be unreasonable.

But, let me be clear. I'm not saying you shouldn't question things—no, certainly not. Knowledge is essential for growth, and questions force us to dig deeper to grasp an understanding. The answers we uncover translate into knowledge, which results in growth. So, then what is it that I'm saying to you? I'm saying accept the fact that you won't have all the answers, but don't use that as an excuse to not believe. The reality is, there are questions we just do not and will not have the answers to on this side of heaven.

The Purpose of the Bible

Sadly, many people reject God simply because they can't explain something in the Bible, or because they find what they refer to as "contradictions." They view the Bible as a puzzle where each piece must perfectly fit to reveal the complete picture before they will accept it as truth. If they believe there's a piece missing or if they can't figure out where one fits, they label the entire thing as defective.

One woman's serious argument against the validity of the Bible was the fact that she found no account of dinosaurs in it. She believed, since there's proof of their existence, at one time, they must have roamed the earth. Therefore, according to her, a record of them should be included in the Bible.

Since the Bible does not explicitly mention dinosaurs, she concluded the entire book must not be true, because if it were, it would include these kinds of historical facts. My friends, this is true ignorance at its best. Although some Bible scholars believe certain passages of Scripture do speak of these prehistoric creatures, allow me to ask this profound question: does it really matter?

For example, if you're studying to be a heart surgeon, what benefit is it to you if your textbook mentions things that have nothing to do with heart surgery—such as, let's say, planting flowers? What purpose would that have other than to sidetrack and distract you from what you need to know to save lives?

Many people are confused about what the Bible is and what it's for. I've heard it referred to as "an idea," "just a tool," "a history book," and "a relic." Some of these descriptions confuse me, and others I find completely absurd, but when I look back on the days before I gave my life to Christ, I realize I had no idea what the purpose of the Bible was either. I guess I thought it was some fancy book meant to decorate the coffee table that the church folk liked to read. But its purpose isn't to teach world history, nor is it for decoration. It is a collection of books written by people of God whose writings were divinely inspired by his Holy Spirit.

When we say "inspired," we mean the words are directly from the mouth of God but written by men. While preserving their unique personalities and writing styles, God worked through these human authors, including their background, cultural context, and research, so that what they wrote was God's inspired Word.[1]

We believe the original writings—the writings of the original authors before copies were made and before translations were completed—are error free. Although minor mistakes have occurred during translation due to human error, the original meaning of the text has not changed. God has the power to preserve his intended message.

Also, it's worth noting that other books were completed during those times by various authors, but through careful consideration, deliberation, and spiritual guidance, only certain books made the cut and earned a place in what we know today as the Bible. The Bible was written to inform, instruct, and encourage.

It informs us of who God is, who we are, and how we can become who God wants us to be. It instructs us on how to live the Christian life according to God's standards, and it encourages us to do that very thing. We believe the Bible is true, and that it contains the pertinent information needed to be saved and to go to heaven. These are the things that are most important.

Willful Unbelief

Some people refuse to believe in God because they can't justify his actions. They decline salvation and forfeit heaven based on their own shallow thoughts, feelings, and perceptions. For example, I've heard many people say something such as, "I just can't believe in a God who condones slavery." And I get where they're coming from. As a new believer, hearing that God gave the nod of approval to

---

1. Duvall and Hays, *Grasping God's Word*.

For the Potential Christian

slavery left me feeling confused and disappointed. I mean, how can such a loving God approve of something so horrific and inhumane as slavery? Still, I chose to trust him. I thought, "Well, I'm sure he had good reason, but even if I don't understand that reason, he's God and I'm not, so that settles it."

However, one day, while reading through the Old Testament, I was greatly troubled in my spirit. There just had to be a good explanation. I was compelled to dig deeper. It was as if God were saying to me, "My child, I don't want you to be troubled. I want you to know the truth." So, I pulled out my spiritual shovel and began to dig. What I uncovered settled the uneasiness in my heart.

You see, as it turns out, slavery in those days was something much different than what we know slavery to be today. As it was used in biblical times, the Hebrew word translated in our English Bibles as "slave" better translates to the word "servant." In those times, people would often sell themselves into slavery to pay off debt or to have their basic needs met, such as food and housing. It was more of an agreement between the slave and his or her owner. At the end of their service, there was even an opportunity for the slave to stay with their master if they chose to.

Therefore, the slavery God speaks of, unlike slavery today, didn't include the kidnapping and forcing of an individual to perform work or acts against their will, while receiving barbarous treatment. As a matter of fact, kidnapping a man and selling him is condemned in the Bible and was even punishable by death.[2] That's how serious of a crime it was. Although this was an Old Testament law, it's also condemned in the New Testament.[3]

The truth is, God always has, and always will, see slavery as it is today as wrong. But how many people who claim slavery as an exemption from serving God take the time to search for that truth? It leads one to wonder: is it their accusation against God that causes them to not believe, or is it their willful unbelief that causes them to settle for ignorance and not seek the truth? In other words, is it because God condones slavery that they refuse to

2. Exod 21:16.
3. 1 Tim 1:9–10.

A Side Note

believe? Or is it because they don't want to believe, so they use the slavery thing as an excuse to continue in sin, not wishing to hear anything that might change their mind? Most often, it's the latter. If a person doesn't want to believe, they won't try to understand.

If they enjoy a destructive lifestyle, what incentive is there to find a reason to turn away from it? Why seek the truth if you're comfortable living with the lie? Isn't it easier to find a flaw in God then cry, "I don't believe!" to justify the continuation of wrongdoing? Why not cover your eyes and ears to protect yourself from the truth so you can enjoy immoral pleasure without feeling bad about it? That would be the easiest thing to do, right? But if we're truly seeking God, there's something in us that instinctively searches for truth, and if our hearts are sincere, he can and will lead us to that truth. He does not want us to be ignorant. He will help us to know the truth and to understand it.

Examine Your Unbelief

So, be careful not to fall in the crowd of skeptics who are quick to raise a brow and diminish the Word of God, simply because they don't understand or have all the answers. Also, take a moment to evaluate any unbelief you may have. Do you sincerely have concerns? Or are your desires holding your mind in a prison of willful ignorance because you fear the truth will change you? Because you're afraid it will change everything you've ever known and take away everything you find pleasurable? This is something only you can answer, and I encourage you to do so honestly, as your soul is at stake. If your unbelief is a result of your lust for worldly things, then I pray your eyes will be opened to what really matters.

But, if you do have honest concerns, I simply plead with you: do not close your heart. Leave it cracked just a little, and be open to receive the truth of God—even if you have doubts. And, think about this: when you were a small child, did you know everything there was to know about your parents or your guardian? No, you didn't. That's because they didn't share every little thing with you. After all, some things weren't any of your business and other things

For the Potential Christian

you wouldn't have understood even if they had explained them to you.

Neither did you know the reason behind every instruction, yet you trusted your parents because in your newly developing mind you didn't know any better, and in your innocent heart you believed they would protect you, guide you, and do what was best for you. You knew everything you needed to know. You didn't receive an explanation for everything, nor did you ask for every little detail, because you had faith in your caretakers. You trusted, loved, and obeyed them, even without all the answers. And you turned out okay, right? So, how much more should you trust a loving Father in heaven who only wants what's best for you?

During our time together, my desire is that you would take on the mind of a young child. Innocent. Uncorrupted. Unpersuaded by arguments, opinions, or prejudice—just a fresh clean slate. As much as it is possible, try to recreate that childlike faith you once possessed as a kid. Matthew 18:3 says that unless we turn and become as little children, we cannot enter into the kingdom of heaven. Unless we become humble, sincere, and teachable as a little child, we can have no place in God's kingdom, as we'd be sure to let our thoughts, emotions, and desires get in the way of belief.

I'm not asking you to blindly follow a religion just because you're told to do so. What I'm asking is that you throw out the excuses and simply give God a chance. Even the smallest morsel of belief opens the door for him to step in and make himself real to you. He will place undeniable evidence in your heart that will prove to you who he is. You may not know how you know, but, trust me, you will know. You will have no doubt in your heart that it's God. I pray the Lord will give you spiritual eyes to see, spiritual ears to hear, and a heart to understand the truth. Okay, now that we've taken care of that business, let's continue.

A Side Note

indeed, if you call out for insight and cry aloud for understanding, and if you look for it as for silver and search for it as for hidden treasure, then you will understand the fear of the Lord and find the knowledge of God. For the Lord gives wisdom; from his mouth come knowledge and understanding.[4]

---

4. Prov 2:3–6 NIV.

— CHAPTER 3 —

What Is Faith?

FIRST, LET'S DISCUSS WHAT faith is not. Faith is not a mystical feeling we get when we close our eyes real tight and wish really hard. Neither does having faith consist of emitting powerful brain waves that mysteriously make something happen when we focus our minds on it. Faith is not equivalent to hope, and, despite popular belief, biblical faith is not blindly believing in something when there's no logical evidence to support its existence.

Rather, to have faith in something or someone means to have total trust or confidence in it or them. "Trust" means to have a solid belief in the character, reliability, truth, strength, or ability of something or someone. It's having a sense of security in that person or thing. Biblical faith is trust in the person of Jesus, the truth of his teaching, and the fact that he redeemed us when he died on the cross at Calvary.[1] It's having complete confidence that he is able, and that he is faithful to make good on his promises, and it involves a total commitment to him as the Lord of our lives.[2]

Before we can trust God, we must acknowledge that he exists. For whatever reason, this is a problem for some people. Many struggle to believe in God, and one of the main arguments I hear from unbelievers is that there's no proof of his existence. This

---

1. Bryant, *Zondervan Compact Bible Dictionary*, 169.
2. Bryant, *Zondervan Compact Bible Dictionary*, 169.

What Is Faith?

would be a valid argument, but the problem with this reasoning is that no matter your worldview, it's going to require some type of faith in something that can't be proven.

The fact is, none of us were around at the beginning of creation, so none of us can be certain of anything. However, we can form an intelligent conclusion based on our knowledge and experiences. I believe faith involves evaluating the evidence of something we can't see, and then making a decision whether or not to accept that something to be real or true based on the available evidence. Consider you and me, for example. Look at how our parts work harmoniously together to sustain life. Even the smallest cell has an important function. Each breath is right on time, and our heart beats to a consistent rhythm to keep us alive.

Could you imagine if we were randomly thrown together? What if our feet happened to be where our hands are and vice versa? What if our noses were on our lips and our eyes on our elbows? None of that would make any sense, would it? But instead, each member of our body has been placed in a specific location, to carry out a specific function. The human body is an amazing thing. We're even designed with special features such as dilating pupils that allow us to see better in the dark.

So, when we take these things into account, can we intelligently conclude that we were created by chance? By some random act of an inanimate universe? I don't know about you, but, based on the evidence nature has revealed to me, I believe I was intentionally handcrafted by a wise and skilled Master Artist. Surely, there was some thought put into my development. But thought can only come from one with an ability to think, and the ability to think can only come from one who is alive. God is alive. Therefore, based on the evidence I *can* see, I believe in what—or who—I *can't* see, which is God.

For the Potential Christian

Why Do We Need Faith in God?

Our relationship with God is dependent upon our faith in him. That's because there's no way we can please him without it.[3] Think about it: how would you feel if someone you loved didn't trust you? You would still love them, but would you be pleased? Of course not. You would be hurt, disappointed, and maybe a little angry. So, why should we expect anything different from God—in whose image we were created? The importance of faith is stressed throughout the Bible in both the Old and New Testaments. Beside the fact that it's commanded of us, why is it so important that we have faith in the Lord?

Let's visit the Scriptures for a moment. One Day, Jesus entered a placed called Capernaum. After he'd been there several days, word spread that he was in town, and immediately people swarmed the house where he was staying. They filled the house until there was no more room—not even by the door. As Jesus preached God's Word, four men came to him carrying a bed. On the bed lay a paralyzed man looking for a miracle.

Unfortunately, the man and his entourage couldn't get close to Jesus because of the crowd, so they decided to go another route. They uncovered the roof where Jesus was and lowered the man's bed down to him. When Jesus saw their faith, he was so impressed that he healed the paralyzed man. He told the man to get up, pick up his bed, and go to his own house. Immediately, the man got up and did everything he was told. Everyone who saw it was amazed and glorified God.[4]

The Lord is pleased when we believe in him. Our faith moves him to work wonders on our behalf and he marvels at the confidence we have in him. Faith unlocks the blessings of God. It's like saying to him, "Lord, I know you're able" and, "God, I believe you'll do what you've promised." And then, it's watching. It's waiting. It's pressing in and expecting the glorious appearance of that

---

3. Heb 11:6.
4. Mark 2:1–12

wonderful promise—his perfect promise, delivered in his perfect time, and in his perfect way.

Faith in Action

Faith moves us to act. It's what thrusts us into motion. Let's look at an example. If you make your living working for someone else, your trust in your employer leads you to perform work on their behalf, because you know you'll be compensated for it. Otherwise, let's face it: you wouldn't work for free. Unless, of course, you're that awesome type of person. But the rest of us do it because we have faith in our employer, and because we're confident in their ability to pay us. Because of this, we know they'll mail, hand-deliver, or deposit into our accounts a well-earned check, bright and early on payday. We don't stop to question whether they'll give it to us or not. We simply expect it.

In like manner, our trust in the Lord leads us to perform certain actions that allow us to receive his blessings. Let's see this played out. In the ninth chapter of John's Gospel, we see Jesus leaving the temple. He'd just slipped away from a crowd who wanted to stone him, when he came across a man who was blind from birth. The man was a beggar who may have been panhandling as Jesus walked by.

For some reason, this poor beggar caught the Lord's attention and he decided to do something about his condition. When Jesus saw the man, he did something unusual. He spat on the ground and made mud with his saliva. Then, he smeared the mud across the man's eyes and instructed him to go wash in a pool. This man had no clue what was going on, but because he believed and trusted Jesus, he did as he was told and washed in the pool of Siloam. As a result, the Bible tells us, he came back seeing![5]

There was another time when Jesus met a man with a withered hand. He had just entered a synagogue—a place where Jewish people gather for religious worship—and there were certain men

---

5. John 9:1–7.

looking to accuse him of breaking the law. They asked him if it was legal to heal people on the Sabbath day, since the Sabbath was to be a day of rest. After Jesus kindly put them in their place, he told the man to stretch out his withered hand. Since the man trusted Jesus, he stretched out his hand, and when he did it was restored—just as complete as the other![6]

But, what if the blind man hadn't trusted Jesus? What if he'd slapped away his hand when he tried to put the mud on his eyes? I can imagine he felt vulnerable, since he was blind and couldn't see what was going on. Wouldn't you think he'd be asking questions as he felt that squishy mud touch the surface of his eyelids? I can just imagine if it were me. I would have probably said something like, "Whoa, wait a minute, Jesus. What is this you're putting on my eyes? I'm sorry, did you say *mud*? It's made of *what!*? Thanks, but *no* thanks!"

And what if the man with the withered hand hadn't trusted him either? Instead of doing what Jesus told him, what if he had responded with ridicule, saying, "Are you out of your mind? Can you not see my hand? How exactly am I supposed to *stretch* it out, Jesus?" then walked away offended and shaking his head in disbelief? Because of his lack of faith, he would have missed out on his miracle.

But the amazing thing about these two men is this: even though they didn't understand what was going on, they chose to believe in the Lord. And because they believed, they trusted, and because they trusted, they obeyed. As a result, they received the healing they so desperately needed. The Lord is trustworthy. We can believe him. All things are possible to the one who believes.

Where Do We Get Faith?

By now you may be wondering, "Okay, so where do I get this good ole faith you've been pumping me up about?" Well, again, faith is equal to trust. We all place trust in many people and many things,

---

[6]. Matt 12:9–13.

What Is Faith?

every day. A toddler taking his first steps trusts his mother to catch him before he falls. Young children trust their parents to provide for them and to take care of them daily. Passengers on a plane have faith in their pilot's ability to get them to their destination safely. And whenever I step onto a crosswalk in Manhattan, I trust the impatient drivers to obey the traffic light so I'm not run over like in a game of Frogger.

We all have the ability to exercise faith, however, the Bible tells us that biblical faith comes from hearing the Word of God.[7] We can't trust in something we've never heard about. Therefore, the first step in producing faith is to hear the Gospel, which is the message about Jesus's death, burial, and resurrection. When we hear God's Word, something amazing happens. His Word passes through our physical ears and penetrates deep down into our spirits. It really shakes something up in there. It's like being in a deep sleep and someone keeps annoyingly nudging you to get up, but you keep pushing them away—until finally you wake up.

God's Word nudges us and screams, "Wake up! I have so much in store for you! Don't let these amazing promises pass you by!" When we believe the Gospel message and respond to it favorably, biblical faith is produced. Faith initially comes from hearing the Gospel of Jesus Christ and responding to it for salvation, but as we saw with the blind man and the man with the withered hand, it doesn't become useless after we're saved. Many more of God's promises are accessible through faith!

As you continually trust God and follow his Word, you'll begin to see these promises manifest in your life. As you do, your faith will be strengthened, and pretty soon you'll be flexing those faith muscles all over the place. The only thing you need to get started is faith the size of a tiny seed. God's Word will nourish it and help it to grow. It's a growing faith!

> Now faith is confidence in what we hope for and assurance about what we do not see. This is what the ancients were commended for. By faith we understand that the

---

7. Rom 10:17 NLT.

universe was formed at God's command, so that what is seen was not made out of what was visible.[8]

---

8. Heb 11:1–3 NIV.

— Chapter 4 —

The One True God

Some define "God" as spiritual energy or an invisible force that holds the universe together. Others believe God exists in every created thing, such as trees, water, people, animals, etc. Many worship carved images, humans, or animals as gods; some say God is a scientific particle; and others believe we're all gods within ourselves. It's "our divine self," as they call it. As you can see, "God" means different things to different people. That's why I find it necessary to begin with the absolute basics, to ensure you and I are on the same page.

So, let's first define the term "God." The *Oxford Dictionary* defines God as "a superhuman being or spirit worshiped as having power over nature or human fortunes."[1] This definition best describes gods believed to have control over water, love, air, etc. An example of these would be the Greek gods—Zeus, Artemis, and the rest of the gang. Other definitions include "any person characterized by greatness or power,"[2] "an adored, admired, or influential person,"[3] and "any person who is strong and capable."[4]

Does Hercules come to mind? How about the comic book heroes you loved as a kid? What about your favorite celebrity, or

1. Lexico.com, s.v. "God." https://www.lexico.com/en/definition/god.
2. "God," in Kohlenberger, *NIV Exhaustive Bible Concordance*, 1363.
3. Lexico.com, s.v. "God." https://www.lexico.com/en/definition/god.
4. "God," in Kohlenberger, *NIV Exhaustive Bible Concordance*, 1363.

the person in your life whom you idolize? The truth is, anyone or anything we worship that influences our thoughts, actions, and opinions can be considered our God. In the book of 2 Corinthians, the Bible even calls Satan a god. He is called "the god of this world,"[5] meaning he has power and influence in the earth, namely, over unbelievers.

Now, let's look at a final definition, which states that God is "the creator and ruler of the universe and source of all moral authority; the supreme being."[6] This definition better fits the God of Christianity. We believe the God of the Bible, or Yahweh, holds all power and authority in his hands. He is the only living and only wise deity. He is the Most High God; therefore, we worship him as such.

The One True God

So, as you can see, because of differing worldviews, there can be as many different gods as there are people. But here is the reality: there can be only one true God. Everyone's view of God can't be correct, as one's idea would surely contradict another's beliefs. No two gods can hold the title of "supreme being." So then, which god is the real God? In 1 Kings 18, the Bible recounts how a prophet named Elijah—a proclaimer of the Word of God—dealt with this very question.

In those days there was a famine, and the people had turned from Yahweh to worship other gods. One day, Elijah instructed the evil king of Israel, Ahab, to gather everyone together to meet him at the top of Mount Carmel. On top of the mountain, Elijah stood alone as the only prophet of the Lord, however, the prophets of Baal—the god whom the people worshiped—were numbered at 450 men.

Elijah told the people to decide for themselves who the real God was and to follow him—whether it be the Lord or whether it

---

5. 2 Cor 4:4 KJV.
6. Lexico.com, s.v. "God." https://www.lexico.com/en/definition/god.

The One True God

be Baal. To assist them with this decision, Elijah called for a test to be done with two bulls. The prophets of Baal were to choose one of the bulls, cut it into pieces, then lay it on wood without setting a fire under it. Elijah would prepare the remaining bull in the same manner. They agreed to take turns calling on their gods, and whichever answered by fire would be the true God.

So, the prophets of Baal went first. They prepared the bull and called upon their god from morning until noon, but there was no answer. They leaped upon the altar they'd made, danced around and cut themselves; they cried out to their god but saw no fire. No one answered, no one listened, and no one cared. Imagine how disappointing that must have been.

Now, it was Elijah's turn. He told the people to come close, so they came near. He took twelve stones and used them to build an altar to the Lord, then he cut the bull into pieces and laid the parts on the wood. Next, he gave instructions to fill four barrels with water, and had the water poured over the sacrifice as well as over the wood. He had this done three times. There was so much water that it filled a trench he'd made around the altar. There could be no mistake about it: the entire thing was soaked.

After everything was in place, Elijah called on the God of Abraham, Isaac, and Israel, and the fire of the Lord fell from heaven. It consumed the bull, the wood, the stones, and the dust. The fire even "licked up" all the water that was in the trench. Now that's a powerful God! When the people saw this, they fell on their faces and chanted, "The Lord, he is the God; the Lord, he is the God."[7]

But what led them to make such a confession? What turned them toward the Lord and away from Baal? It was the fact that they had an experience with the living God. He was put to the test and proved himself to be who he claimed to be, which is the true God. These days, we probably won't see God annihilate a bull with heavenly fire, but he still has ways of proving he's real. Everyone's experience will be different because he knows our specific needs. He knows how to create a personalized experience to effectively reveal himself to each individual.

7. 1 Kgs 18:16–39 KJV.

For the Potential Christian

As Christians, we believe the God of the Bible is God alone. We call him Jehovah, Yahweh, Adonai, and El Shaddai, among various other names and titles. He is the God of Christ and the God of Abraham, Isaac, and Jacob. All others are false gods—period, point blank, end of discussion. So, now that we've determined there's one real God and who he is, we can rightly answer questions about his character and nature.

God Is Spirit

Thanks to certain paintings and cartoons, many imagine God as an old man with a long white robe and a matching white beard, who lives on a cloud in the sky. It may sound silly to some, but to be honest, none of us fully understand who God is. However, we can learn a lot from what he reveals about himself in his Word.

Let me first take a moment to clear up some common clichés. Regardless of what you've heard, God is not "The Big Guy in the Sky" and he's not "The Man Upstairs." In fact, he's not a man at all. The Bible tells us that "God is a Spirit,"[8] which means he's an invisible being with no physical shape or form.

We can't see God with our natural eyes, but once we give our lives to Christ, we receive an additional set of eyes—spiritual eyes. This new sight allows us to see the Lord at work all around us. Because he is a "spirit," God has no boundaries or physical limitations, which, as we'll discuss later, is of great benefit to us.

Creator and Sustainer

Most have a general knowledge of God and accept the fact that he created the universe. God is indeed the Creator and Sustainer of all things.[9] He's the only being in the history of the world who has ever made something out of nothing. When he began to speak, things began to exist. Whenever he said, "Let there be . . . ,"

---

8. John 4:24 KJV.
9. Col 1:16–17.

The One True God

something became so. In the first chapter of the book of Genesis, we're given a rundown of how he established the entire universe in only six days.

He made the sun, the moon, the stars, the trees, the waters, and all the grass. He made every animal, including those that walk on land and those that swim in the sea. All creatures that creep in the dirt, as well as those that soar in the air, were designed by him. And of course, he made us—human beings. Mankind was made separate and unique from the rest of creation. God made us in his image and personally breathed life into us.[10] He placed us higher than all earthly beasts, plants, and non-living things.

I guess you could say we're the centerpiece of this magnificent work of art called "creation." The world was intentionally designed with us in mind. That's why I don't accept the idea that things were randomly formed, because as we can see, "in creation, there is order, there is purpose, and there is meaning."[11] These things don't come by chance. No man has seen God, yet wherever we look the evidence of an intelligent Creator is all around us. If you don't believe me, just look outside.

Around the same time each morning, the sun shines its light so we can work during the day, then gracefully bows out to allow the moon to come and give us a time of rest. The sky, land, and seas dwell in separate compartments so one doesn't get in the way of the other, and the seasons change in the same order, every year, without fail.

If someone with wisdom beyond our own wasn't behind all of this, there would be complete chaos. But instead, we see consistent order throughout creation. We see everything operating in a decent and organized fashion, and with a purpose. With these things in mind, does it make sense to believe this elaborate stage called "earth" was not purposefully and thoughtfully designed, but came about by happenstance?

---

10. Gen 2:7.
11. Holsteen and Svigel, *Exploring Christian Theology*, 31.

For the Potential Christian

The Bible states that in the beginning God created the heavens and the earth and the earth was empty and without form.[12] It was in a state of disorganization. Have you ever seen a construction site for a building? Picture the building materials lying on the ground. There is no structure, function, or order to the pile of matter. It would take a wise and skilled builder to shape it, mold it, and turn it into something useful. Now, if that's true for a building, would it not be the same, and even more so, for this awesome and complex world we inhabit?

Before the first seed was planted and before anything grew, the Lord gave fruit. Before the first baby was formed in the wall of a mother's womb, the Lord gave life. By his Word, he called everything into existence and shaped it into the world we live in today. All of creation was made by him, for him. He is not a part of it, but he exists outside of it. Even so, he's still very much active in it.

Self-Existent, Holy, and Eternal

Yes, God created all things, yet he was created by nothing and no one. He is what we call "self-existent." No one can explain his existence, and no oldest genealogy record tells us "who begat whom" to bring him into a state of being. He just is, and he's always been since before the beginning of time, since of course he created time. He's in a category of his own. That's what makes him holy.

The word "holy," as it pertains to the Almighty God, means he is separate and distinct from all of creation. It means he is perfect in goodness and righteousness and there is no speck of evil in him. He is completely pure. Although our holiness is far beneath his, God calls his children to be holy since he is holy,[13] which means we should separate ourselves from sinful living.

God is also eternal. This means he has no beginning and no end. We can describe the life of a man in three stages: he is born, he lives, and he dies. But when describing our Maker's existence,

---

12. Gen 1:1–2.
13. 1 Pet 1:15–16.

The One True God

the only one that applies is *he lives*. He has no point of origin or termination. He doesn't dwell within space and time, but he exists inside of eternity. He is the Alpha and the Omega, which means he is the beginning and the end of all things.[14] Everything starts and ends with God.

If all of creation were to disappear tomorrow, guess what? The Lord would still be. There's been nothing and no one before him; neither will anything nor anyone come to take his place. He is it. He is God. There is none higher and there is none greater. So, write it down and make a note of it: God answers to no one. It can be hard for our finite minds to grasp this truth, but it's one of those things we have to believe in faith.

But, if you think about it, the truth that God has no beginning or end isn't that hard to believe. In fact, we've all held a similar belief before. Here's what I mean. From the time you were born up until you reached a certain age, you didn't know where your parents came from, did you? Before intellect spoiled the innocence of your faith, you didn't even think to question it. You knew nothing about the "birds and the bees" and hadn't the faintest idea that your parents were once babies themselves.

You didn't know how they existed; you only knew that they were there, and that they took care of you—and that was enough. We may not know all the details surrounding God's presence, but what we know for sure is this: he exists, he loves us, and he always has and always will be there for his beloved children.

> Jesus answered, "I tell you the truth, before Abraham was even born, I am!"[15]

The Triple Os

God has several characteristics that set him apart from creation. There are three specific attributes of God, which I like to refer to as the "Triple Os." He is omnipresent, omnipotent, and omniscient.

14. Rev 1:8.
15. John 8:58 NLT.

For the Potential Christian

The prefix *omni-* comes from the Latin word meaning "all," so when we say God is "omnipresent," we mean he is all-present. To put it in simpler terms, it means he's everywhere at the same time.

Just as air is present where I am right now, but also where you are, so is the presence of God. He can be a friend to you and a comforter to me at the same time. It's amazing, right? God is not confined to the sky, although in our small imaginations we tend to hold him captive there. He has no bounds; therefore, he cannot be held in any amount of space. He's everywhere.

It's a good thing too because that means we have a God who is never too busy for us and is always there when we need him. He's a very present help during our times of trouble, and we can each have his undivided attention at any time. How many others can we say that about? Whether with a loud desperate cry or a soft weak whisper, when we call on him for help, he's already there.

In addition to being omnipresent, God is also omnipotent; he's all-powerful. You may remember this song growing up: "He's got the whole world, in his hands. He's got the whole wide world, in his hands. He's got the whole world, in his hands. He's got the whole world in his hands." Just be thankful you only had to read that and didn't have to hear me sing it—never could hold a tune.

But, it's true. God's got the whole world in his hands and the entire universe bends to his will. Consider how he only spoke the words "Let there be light" and light came into existence.[16] He placed the sun and the moon in their respective places, and the seas don't dare go beyond the boundaries he's set for them. Even the wind and the waves obey him.[17]

All power belongs to him. He has the power to change minds and the power to change hearts[18]—the power to build up and the power to tear down. Without strength or force, he caused a great wall to come crashing down around the city of Jericho.[19] Almost

---

16. Gen 1:3.
17. Matt 8:23–27.
18. Ezek 36:26.
19. Josh 6:20.

The One True God

everyone has heard how he turned water into wine.[20] And who can forget the time he enabled a barren woman to give birth to her first child at the ripe old age of ninety?[21] He's healed the sick,[22] raised the dead,[23] and everything else in between. There is nothing too hard for the Lord. He has the power to do anything that is consistent with his character, and one thing he can never do is fail. There is no power higher than the Almighty God. His power is limitless.

Now, revisit your childhood again for a moment. Think of a time when you did something you weren't supposed to but managed to get away with it by hiding it from your parents. Do you remember the feeling of victory that swept over you when you found out you were in the clear? Do you recall that moment of relief when you realized you'd escaped certain punishment? Well, that isn't happening with God. That's because he's what we call "omniscient," which means he is all-knowing. He knows everything, so you're never going to pull a fast one on him.

No one has instructed the Lord, but he has perfect knowledge of all things. In Isaiah 46:9-10, God declares, ". . . I am God, and there is no other; I am God, and no one is like Me. I declare the end from the beginning . . ." He knows the end from the beginning because he holds the pen in his hand and is the author of each of our stories. He knows every past, present, and future. He knows every thought, hope, and desire. He knows the length of our days on earth, the number of hairs on our heads,[24] and the ultimate plan for our lives. God knows when we're troubled, he sees when we're hurting, and he knows how to lift us up and encourage us. Today, if you're seeking him with a sincere heart, trust me—he knows that too. And he will reward you.

---

20. John 2:1-11
21. Gen 17:16-17.
22. Matt 8:14-15.
23. Mark 5:35-43.
24. Matt 10:30.

For the Potential Christian

God Doesn't Change

In Malachi 3:6, God says, "For I am the Lord, I change not..." It's good to know that, unlike our encounters with people, we don't have to adjust our personalities to fit whatever mood God is in. He is who he is, and he's that all the time. He's good all the time and he's always holy. His character doesn't change and neither does his Word. Since he's not human, he doesn't go back on his promises like we often do.[25] If he said it back then, it's still true today. Therefore, we can take him at his Word. Heaven and earth have a better chance of passing away before even one of God's promises goes unfulfilled.[26]

Another good thing to know is that God's love for us doesn't change. He loves us at the highest level today, and thankfully there's nothing we can do to make him love us less tomorrow. There's also no good deed we can perform to make him love us more next week. His tenderness toward us is steadfast, faithful, and unchanging. He doesn't love as we love.

We generally love and do good to those who love us, and barely tolerate all the others. But the Lord's adoration goes beyond that. It's a love we can't comprehend because it's given without reason or cause. Even when we do bad things, he corrects us, but he still loves us. He lavishes his children with unlimited affection, even though we don't deserve it.

The Bible recounts many instances where God showed love in this manner. One example is seen in the Old Testament when his chosen people, the Israelites, caused him much grief. So many times the children of Israel turned from God, angered him, and broke his heart, yet so many times he embraced them when they cried out to him for forgiveness. Regardless of their constant rebellion (although not without consequences), he made sure they had what they needed. He watched over them and protected them, the same way a father would do, and it's good to know nothing has changed. He still does the same for his children today.

25. Num 23:19.
26. See Matt 24:35.

The One True God

Another thing about God that doesn't change is his power. I once heard a wise preacher say that God doesn't lose power just because he uses it. He didn't use it up long ago, and he's not on the verge of depletion. God's power bank never drains, and never needs a refill or recharge. If he had power to heal in King Hezekiah's day,[27] we can be confident that he can heal our sick and diseased bodies today. And if Jesus could perform miracles over two thousand years ago, he still has power to work a miracle for us in our lifetime.

Best of all, if the Lord had the power to save me, then he still has power to save you too. There is no one outside of his reach. Times change and people change, but God doesn't change. He never has, and he never will. This is a good thing for us because we can rest in the fact that his grace, love, and mercy will always remain the same.

Jesus Christ is the same yesterday, today, and forever.[28]

God Is Love

What comes to your mind when you think about love? Maybe the love between a man and a woman? Perhaps the relationship between a child and a parent? The love shared between lifelong friends or the endearment one shows toward a beloved pet? There are different types of love and many variations of what we consider it to be. But the love of God is unique and is like no other love. In fact, the Bible tells us that God himself is love.[29] Love is not merely an expression or an action he performs, but it's the core of his entire being.

He didn't create us out of necessity because he was lonely and needed someone to talk to, but God in his infinite goodness chose to share himself with us. Although we rebelled against him, he still chose to love us. Can you think of a time when you were building

27. 2 Kgs 20:1–7.
28. Heb 13:8 NKJV.
29. 1 John 4:8.

For the Potential Christian

or creating something you had high hopes for, but for whatever reason it came out horribly wrong?

After you looked over the finished product and noted its many flaws, what did you do? Did you rip it up and throw it away? Did you tear it down and start over? Did you give up on the idea altogether? Or did you try to redeem it? Did you do everything you could to make it work? If you're like me, you probably bulldozed it and thought nothing else about it.

The fact is, we're human. We give up easily, and we throw things away. But God is not like us. You see, when God created humans and saw we were evil, he regretted that he made us. He planned to wipe us off the face of the earth because of our wickedness, but one faithful man, named Noah, found grace in the sight of the Lord.[30]

Because of God's love and Noah's obedience, God preserved his creation instead of destroying it. He decided to keep us. He didn't just give up and throw us away like most of us would have done, but he determined that even though our hearts were wicked we were worth saving. Because of his mercy, God made a plan for our redemption.

That plan included the greatest act of love one could show to another. God sent his only Son, Jesus Christ, to die for our sins. This was truly a loving sacrifice. I mean, think about it. Would you hand your one and only child over to a bloodthirsty mob to be killed for the likes of wicked and evil people? Would you sacrifice one of them if you had ten? Certainly not. "But God demonstrates His own love toward us, in that while we were still sinners, Christ died for us."[31] There is no greater love than that.

> Beloved, let us love one another, for love is from God, and whoever loves has been born of God and knows God. Anyone who does not love does not know God, because God is love.[32]

---

30. Gen 6:5–8.
31. Rom 5:8 NKJV.
32. 1 John 4:7–8 ESV.

— Chapter 5 —

What Is Sin?

S-I-N. It's amazing how a tiny three-letter word can have such power over us. Many people grow tense and drawback when they hear it, and some become offended at the very mention of the word. But, why is that? Why do some try to avoid it like a coworker with the flu? It's because this word, when added to a conversation, can make for a very uncomfortable discussion.

The fact is, most people don't like to talk about it. Before I became a Christian, I didn't want to talk about it either. There was just something about that word that would set off an alarm in my head, alerting me to immediately make a break for it. My mind would suggest a whole host of possible responses. Run away! Change the subject! Act like you didn't hear it! Do anything! Just make the conviction stop!

I didn't want to hear it. I already knew my way of living wasn't pleasing to the Lord—for crying out loud, don't make me feel bad about it too! I didn't want to feel guilty about doing things I knew were wrong. I just wanted to continue my life of sin and not be bothered. Was that too much to ask? Besides, I knew no better way to live. Sin was all I ever knew. But now I understand that it can't be swept under a rug or tiptoed around. It absolutely must be dealt with because it's the one thing that can eternally separate us from God. So, what is sin?

For the Potential Christian

The late, great Billy Graham once answered this question by saying, "A sin is any thought or action that falls short of God's will."[1] So, anything we do or think that doesn't measure up to God's standards is considered sin. *Merriam-Webster's Dictionary* defines sin as being "an offense against a religious or a moral law."[2] Based on this definition, to sin is to break the law of God. It means to err, to be mistaken or incorrect. It means to miss the mark.

In archery, the archer draws back his bow, aims, and then releases his arrow. If he misses the bull's-eye, he misses his target, therefore, he misses the mark. He aimed at perfection but was off by maybe a few inches. This is generally the idea of sin. God is perfect, and his ways are perfect, but we are not. So, we sin when we miss the target of God's perfection.

We miss the mark when we tell that "little lie" instead of the truth and when we give in to that urge to gossip rather than walking away. Sin doesn't only consist of doing things we know we shouldn't do, such as steal, but it also includes not doing things we know we should do, such as forgive. We sin when we fall short of meeting God's holy requirements and when we refuse to obey his commandments.

Everyone has sinned. It's not limited to a group of people with certain characteristics. There are no specific backgrounds, personalities, or demographics that are more prone to sin than others. The Bible informs us in Romans 3:23, "For all have sinned, and come short of the glory of God" (KJV). No one is excluded. The president of the United States, kings and queens from both past and present, millionaires, billionaires, the poor, and commoners alike—we have all sinned. We've all been guilty before the holy and righteous Judge.

---

1. Graham, "Billy Graham: Things God Hates."

2. Merriam-Webster.com, s.v. "sin." https://www.merriam-webster.com/dictionary/sin

What Is Sin?

Man's First Sin

Most of us, regardless of our religious background, have heard of the famous duo Adam and Eve. But just in case you haven't, here's a brief summary. At the beginning of creation, on the sixth day, God created man in his image and placed him in the garden of Eden. The first man, Adam, was permitted by God to freely eat of every tree in the garden, except for the one tree planted in the middle, which was the Tree of the Knowledge of Good and Evil.

God told Adam that the day he ate from that tree he would surely die.[3] Pretty straightforward and to the point, right? If you eat it, you die; if you don't eat it, you don't die—fairly simple rules to understand and follow. So, Adam heeded God's warning and kept away from the tree. After all, he had everything he needed. He had a beautiful wife, there was communion with God every day, and they had an endless supply of fruit. Yes, life was good in the garden. There were no worries, no evil, and no concerns—just good food and good company.

However, one day the conniving serpent, who is Satan, came along toting a suitcase full of deception. His goal was to sell a lie that contradicted what God had already said. He told Eve, Adam's wife, that she could be like God, knowing good and evil, if she ate from the tree. He basically told her not to worry about what God said because it wasn't true. He assured her she would not surely die from simply eating a piece of fruit, but that her eyes would be opened.

Unfortunately, Eve bought the lie. Because of her pride, she was tricked into eating of the tree that God forbade them to eat from. Not only did she eat, but she gave it to Adam and he also ate. Thus, the first sin of man, our first transgression against God, was committed. As a result of their error, the couple was evicted from the garden, and mankind was separated from God. Death, suffering, and evil all became a part of life.

Basically, these two messed it up for everyone. But, though it's easy to throw stones at Adam and Eve for their foolishness,

---

3. Gen 2:16–17.

when we consider all the things in this world God gives us to freely enjoy, yet we engage in the few activities he tells us to stay away from, are we not guilty of the same foolishness? Why do you think that is? Why do we continue to make wrong decisions and willingly go against what we know to be right? It's because of our sinful nature—the one that's been passed down from generation to generation since the first sin of Adam and Eve.

We are all born into sin as a result of what happened in the garden. In other words, we all enter the world with a natural desire to do what is wrong. Let me prove it to you. If you've been around little kids long enough, you've experienced a similar scenario where they take something they aren't supposed to, such as food or candy, then hide somewhere and eat it. Afterward, they lie about it even though you found a trail of candy wrappers leading to their hideout, not to mention the fresh chocolate smudges on their face.

So, how do toddlers know how to steal? How do they know how to lie? Generally, they aren't taught to do these things, but they do them because it's part of their selfish sinful nature, which we each inherited from our first mother and father. Regardless of our gender, personality, social status, or ethnic background, the one characteristic shared by every one of us is our natural instinct to sin.

The Consequences of Sin

God hates sin and he hates what it does to us. I once heard a sermon preached by Billy Graham where he brilliantly illustrates God's hatred for sin:

> I tell you that God hates sin just as a father hates a rattlesnake that threatens the safety and life of his child. God loathes evil and diabolic forces that would pull people down to a godless eternity just as a mother hates a venomous spider that is found playing on the soft, warm flesh of her little baby.[4]

---

4. BGEA, "Billy Graham's Answer: What Is Sin?"

What Is Sin?

God loves us, and doesn't want us harmed by sin. He doesn't want us suffering the effects of it while on earth, and he doesn't want us spending eternity apart from him because of it. However, since God is morally perfect, he cannot allow sin to go unpunished. He is a just judge, and must truthfully separate right and wrong. He must be faithful to who he is, therefore, he must issue reward or punishment accordingly.

It may seem harsh, but what would you think of a society where our justice system allowed everyone to do evil with no consequences? What if there were no governments in place to make clear distinctions between right and wrong? What if there was no one to make and enforce laws? Everyone could get away with murder. If you think the world is a mess now, imagine how chaotic it would be if there were no consequences for crimes, such as rape, murder, and theft. Laws are made for our benefit to protect us, to keep order, and to promote peace.

Just as there are consequences for breaking the laws of man, so are there consequences for breaking the laws of God. If we expect discipline for wrongful actions and require justice for crimes against us, how can we say God is unjust for doing the same? His commandments are not grievous and they're not meant to ruin our fun, but they are to protect us. They protect us from sin's consequences, which are both present and eternal.

We often focus on the afterlife, but sin also effects our present lives. Let me share an example. There was a guy I knew as a kid whose life spiraled down as an adult. He got involved with a gang and unfortunately lost his life to gun violence. He was still very young and in the prime of his life, but sin robbed him of his future. He left behind small children and a newly single mother who now had to do life on her own. Consider how these situations not only affect the individual, but also those closest to them. Sin is a destroyer. It's like cancer. It starts out small and in an isolated area, but as it grows it begins to spread, destroying everything around it.

Although it can wreak havoc in our current lives, the greatest consequence of sin is spending eternity apart from God. I've watched many suspense films where the characters run through a facility trying to escape, when suddenly a huge wall comes flying down out of nowhere and separates them. At that moment, they begin yelling and banging on the wall hysterically, but nothing happens. They can hear nothing; neither can they be heard. They've lost all contact and communication with each other.

Similar to the wall, sin separated us from God when Adam and Eve disobeyed him in the garden. As a result of the fall, mankind became polluted with sin, and we could no longer enjoy sweet fellowship with the Lord since he hates sin. The relationship between creation and Creator was broken, and there was nothing we could do to repair it. Sin is part of our human nature and we're powerless over it. It continuously drives a wedge between us and God. This wedge creates a gap that, if not closed, will result in the loss of our souls.

The Bible tells us that the wages of sin is death.[5] Therefore, if we choose to live our lives, working to do what is evil in God's sight, then in the end we'll receive what we rightfully earned, which is eternal death. There is no hidden or misleading information here. We're told upfront that death and eternal separation from God is what we should expect to receive from a life of sin.

The Lord is pure, clean, and holy, and he will not allow any sin to enter the kingdom of heaven.[6] After all, we can't go around dirtying up the streets of gold with our filthy sin. We must be washed clean by the blood of Jesus Christ so that we become pure and holy in the sight of the Lord. There is no way around it. It's the only way to make it into those pearly gates.

The Remedy for Sin

After Adam and Eve ate the forbidden fruit, their eyes were indeed opened. They could now know what was good and what was evil. Their days of ignorant bliss came to an abrupt end as they suddenly realized they were stark naked. They sewed together fig leaves to

---

5. Rom 6:23.
6. 1 Cor 6:9–10.

What Is Sin?

cover themselves, and unlike before when they freely roamed in their birthday suits, when they heard the voice of the Lord, they hid themselves.

God called to them and asked, "Where are you?" Adam replied and said he hid himself since he was afraid because he was naked. God asked him how he knew he was naked, and asked if he'd eaten from the tree he said not to eat from. After first blaming God and throwing Eve under the bus, saying, "The woman whom You gave to be with me, she gave me of the tree . . . ,"[7] Adam admitted to eating the fruit.

Then, God turned and questioned the woman, but Eve blamed the serpent, saying, "The serpent deceived me, and I ate."[8] God punished the serpent, but as we know, everyone involved suffered consequences for their actions. Each one was held accountable for their own sin. It's no different for us today. Many times we blame others or use bad experiences with church or religion as an excuse to sin, but on the day of judgement each of us will be held accountable for our own actions. No finger-pointing gives us a get-out-of-jail-free card.

But, the good news is, although God punished Adam and Eve for their wrongdoing, he didn't despise them. Instead, he made tunics of animal skins to clothe them, to cover up their nakedness and shame. Although they rebelled against him, he still showed love and compassion toward them. He still offered them grace. He didn't give up on mankind, nor did he stop caring for us because we messed up.

He could have easily tossed us and started over and his actions would have been just. But instead, he had a plan for our redemption. Just as we must all suffer the consequences of Adam's sin and disobedience to God, through another man's *sinless* life and *obedience* to God, we all have the opportunity to be saved from sin and from the consequences of it.

---

7. Gen 3:12.
8. Gen 3:13.

For the Potential Christian

For as by one man's disobedience many were made sinners, so by the obedience of one shall many be made righteous.[9]

---

9. Rom 5:19 NKJV.

— Chapter 6 —

Jesus: The Lamb of God

I'll never forget the moment when I fully surrendered to Jesus Christ. It was a powerful experience that changed my life forever. In the days that immediately followed, I can remember rushing home and eagerly running up the stairs to my little second-floor apartment, grabbing my Bible, and lying in front of the couch to continue through the pages of Matthew.

I couldn't read through those chapters fast enough. I was so hungry for knowledge that at times I would look up and hours would have passed. Sometimes, I would even forget to eat. This was significant because I didn't skip meals—at least not voluntarily. But God's Word commanded my attention and captivated me in such a way that I couldn't step away from it—not even for a moment. I had to find out all I could about this man named Jesus.

I didn't know much about him. As a child, my mother sent us to church most Sundays, so I knew the basic stuff. I heard his name during sermons and Christmas skits and I knew he'd died on a cross, but I didn't really know who he was. I didn't understand what he had done, or why it should even matter to me. The only two things I knew for certain were that his name was Jesus and he died. That's as far as my knowledge went.

Do you know how it is when you know someone but you don't know them? In other words, you've seen them around a few times and may even know their name, but you've never had so much as a brief conversation with them. You know who they are, but you know nothing about them as far as their character, their personality, their likes, or their dislikes.

Well, that's how it was for me. I'd heard of Jesus, but I didn't know him. I'd never met him personally, but as I read through the Gospels—Matthew, Mark, Luke, and John—I started to get to know him in a personal way. I began to grow closer to him and more in love with him with each passage of Scripture. Once I realized how much he loved me—it just blew me away! He became more than just a name to me. He became a close friend.

Now, could I ask you a personal question? Do you know Jesus? I mean do you really know him? If not, then allow me to introduce you to him today. He is strong and fierce, yet meek and mild. He commands demons to flee, but gently leads his sheep. Through him all things were made, and without him nothing was made that exists. He is the King of kings and the Lord of lords—the undefeated Champion and Savior of the entire world. He is the awesome, the mighty, the one and only Jesus Christ! And he desires for you to know him—in a personal way.

The Image of the Invisible God

Jesus of Nazareth, whom we often refer to as Jesus Christ, entered the world through a unique birth. He was supernaturally conceived, born of a virgin woman named Mary, and of the Holy Spirit.[1] He is the Son of God. When we refer to him as the "Son," we don't mean he was conceived through physical means, but that he is of the same nature as God. Everything about him is unique. That's because he's no ordinary man.

Every aspect of his earthly life was significant, from conception to death. But, why is he so special? Well, for starters, he is the Redeemer of mankind. Despite popular belief, Christ is not Jesus's last name, but it's a title that means "the anointed one," "the chosen

---

1. Luke 1:26–38.

Jesus: The Lamb of God

one," or "Messiah." So, essentially, when we say "Jesus Christ," we're saying, "Jesus the anointed one" or "Jesus the Messiah."

The word "messiah" generally refers to someone who is a leader or savior of a specific group or cause. Jesus was the promised Savior,[2] chosen to come to earth to save his people from their sins.[3] Now, you may ask, "What do you mean he was chosen to come to earth? Where did he come from?" The answer is, he came from heaven. He existed before the world began.

Do you remember when I said God is invisible and has no physical form but that he is a Spirit? Well, Jesus is the image of the invisible God,[4] meaning he is the physical representation of God the Father, whom we cannot see. He is God in the flesh, being fully human and fully God at the same time. Just as air is made manifest inside a balloon, so was the invisible God manifested in the man Jesus Christ. Quite simply, Jesus is all the qualities of God bottled up inside of a human body. So, why did God come to earth as a man?

Let's start with a little background information. As I stated before, because God is just, he cannot allow sin to go unpunished. Therefore, whenever sin is committed, payment will be required. The payment for sin is death. Before Jesus entered the world, the only way people could have their sin pardoned was to offer an animal sacrifice to take their place. It was basically a trade-off—the innocent for the guilty.

But the problem with this method was that it wasn't a permanent fix. The people didn't have power to stop sinning, and every time they did, they had to kill an innocent animal to cover their wrong. Now, you may think, "Well, that's not fair to the animals," and I certainly would agree with you. But neither was it fair for Jesus, the innocent Lamb of God, to have to suffer and die for our sins so we could be free. Nevertheless, if he hadn't done it, we would be lost for all eternity.

---

2. Isa 42:6–7.
3. Matt 1:21.
4. Col 1:12–15.

For the Potential Christian

Since we are all born into sin, none of us qualify to save ourselves. Only an innocent life can pay for sin, and God alone is sinless. He's the only one who is truly good. Therefore, he set it up so he could come to earth and take our punishment for us. The animal thing was only temporary, but God's plan all along was to offer himself as the ultimate and final sacrifice for sin. That's why he took on the form of human flesh and died on a cross. As a result, animal sacrifices are no longer needed, but only faith in Jesus Christ.

Of course, some argue that Jesus is not God in the flesh, however, the Bible provides much evidence to support the opposite. Here's an example. When one of Jesus's disciples asked him to show them the Father, Jesus answered by saying that anyone who has seen him has seen the Father. He made it known on multiple occasions that he is in the Father and the Father is in him.[5]

Additionally, in John 10, Jesus declared that he and the Father are one.[6] In those days, a statement like that would get you more than dirty looks and psychiatric treatment referrals. It would place you next in line for a good stoning. So, when the Jews picked up stones to kill Jesus, he questioned their reason. They said they were stoning him for blasphemy since he, being a mere man, made himself equal to God. The interesting thing is that Jesus didn't deny their claim, nor did he attempt to correct them. He wouldn't allow them to think such a thing, if it were false.

So, Christ himself claimed to be God. Therefore, if we believe the Scriptures to be God's Word, and if we believe God's Word is true, then we should believe what the Lord has spoken in his Word. Jesus is God. He is the second person in what we refer to as the "Trinity," which is made up of God the Father, God the Son, and God the Holy Spirit. As a three-leaf clover consists of three parts within one unit, we worship one God who consists of three persons—Father, Son, and Spirit.

Though God the Father is invisible, we can see what he's like by looking at his Son, Jesus. Christ embodies the character,

---

5. John 14:8–10.
6. John 10:30.

qualities, and love of the Father. The Lord loved us so much that he left his glorious throne to rescue us from a miserable eternity. Like Superman suits up to go forth and save the day, God, in his humility, suited up in human flesh to come to earth and save souls. Now, there's a *real* hero.

> "Behold, the virgin shall be with child, and bear a Son, and they shall call His name Immanuel," which is translated, "God with us."[7]

He Walked Among Us

On one hand, Jesus lived a normal life while on earth. He belonged to a loving family that consisted of a mother, father, brothers, and sisters, and he had friends whom he cared for deeply. He worked as a carpenter to pay bills, and he usually walked wherever he went. He wasn't rich, he was plain-looking, and according to popular belief he may have been homeless at one point. Jesus regularly enjoyed meals with friends, he faithfully attended worship services, and he took part in festivals and weddings.

He was kind and gentle, yet spoke with great strength and authority. Though he had divine power, he was subject to the laws of human nature. He still needed food to survive, his body required regular sleep and rest, and he could physically be in only one place at a time. Also, like us, he had to deal with his feelings. The Lord experienced emotions such as joy, sadness, anger, and grief, so he can sympathize with our pain and relate to our struggles because he knows how it feels.

Let's stop for a moment and think about this: God could have chosen any form to reveal himself to us. He could have come in great power and glory and demanded to be worshiped, but instead he chose the likeness of weak, fragile man so he could learn to identify with us. He's a compassionate Savior who is very in touch with humanity.

---

7. Matt 1:23 NKJV.

For the Potential Christian

In his life, Christ experienced hardship and temptation as we do, yet unlike us he did not sin—ever. Therefore, he invites his followers to come boldly to him in prayer, to receive help in times of trouble. He's been there before, so he knows exactly what we need.

Now, on the other hand, when Jesus walked the earth, he performed many miracles. He healed the sick, raised the dead, and turned water into wine. He prepared an all-you-can-eat buffet with two fish and five loaves of bread. And who hasn't heard how he walked on water as if it were a shag carpet on the living room floor?

He taught his disciples how to live pleasing to God, and he shared many secrets about the kingdom of heaven. He accomplished a lot in his thirty-three years, but his greatest work was completed when he hung on a cross and died for our sins. Because he died, we have an opportunity to live and to be set free from sin.

Our Substitution

Jesus suffered ridicule, rejection, and pain for us. Remember, the wages of sin is death, so since we have all sinned, we all deserve to die. However, Jesus died in our place. Here's how it went down. Judas Iscariot, one of the Lord's trusted disciples, betrayed him for a measly thirty pieces of silver. He gave Jesus up to those who wanted to kill him.

When the mob came to take Jesus, the rest of his disciples—the ones he should have been able to count on—fled and abandoned him. He was left all alone with those who demanded his blood. Can you imagine how he must have felt in that moment? Nevertheless, he didn't run, hide, or fight, but he stood firm. He knew this was part of the mission; for this reason he had come. After they seized Jesus, they led him away like a criminal wanted for murder.

He was questioned, humiliated, and falsely accused. When the people were given a choice of which prisoner they wanted released, they yelled for Barabbas, a murderer, to be freed instead of

Jesus: The Lamb of God

Jesus, the one who knew no sin. The one who healed their sick and fed them fish when they were hungry. The one who came to give life, but whom they sentenced to death.

Although they found no reason to charge him, the people yelled, "Crucify him! Crucify him!" And so, the quiet and humble Jesus was sentenced to death. And presumably, thirty-nine lashes were laid into his back. In agony and torment, Christ, the gentle Lamb of God, endured horrible pain, as pieces of flesh were ripped from his body with every strike of the whip.

Afterward, they stripped him down. They put a robe on his back, a crown of thorns on his head, and mocked him, saying, "Hail, King of the Jews!" He was beaten and spat upon. He was shamed and cast out. Then, as a lamb led to the slaughter, they led him away to be crucified. He remained quiet and protested not as he carried his cross on his mutilated back. He was weak and out of breath, with hardly enough strength to stand.

He must have been so close to the point of death that his executors felt the need to recruit a man, named Simon, to carry his cross for him. At any time he could have prayed to the Father to send more than twelve legions of angels to rescue him,[8] but instead he kept walking—for us. Finally, they came to a place called Golgotha, or Calvary, and it was there where the Lord of Glory was crucified. It was there where they attached him to the cross by driving nails into his upper and lower extremities.

It was at Calvary where he hung on a tree, hanging by only the flesh of his hands and feet. He may have struggled to see as blood ran down his face and into his eyes, resulting from the thorny crown digging into his scalp. He was in excruciating pain and amazing anguish, yet he spoke not a word against his murderers. Instead, he prayed for them, saying, "Father, forgive them for they do not know what they are doing."[9]

Then, heaven began to mourn. Darkness fell down and covered the entire land beginning at the sixth hour and lasting until the ninth. In all this time, Jesus remained faithfully on the cross.

8. Matt 26:53.
9. Luke 23:34 NIV.

For the Potential Christian

They say he could have come down if he wanted to—but that if he had, he would have lost us. He had us on his mind, therefore, he chose to hang on because he couldn't let us go. He chose to suffer and endure the pain.

Suddenly, those nearby heard Jesus cry, "My God, my God, why have you forsaken me?"[10] Then, after someone ran and got him a drink, Jesus uttered his final words: "Father, into Your hands I commit My spirit"[11] and "It is finished."[12] Then, he died. He willingly and graciously paid the price for our sins with his life. He took our place on the cross, and underwent a horrible death that each one of us should have had to face.

After he was crucified, his body was taken and placed inside of a tomb. But, the story doesn't end there. Three days later, God raised him from the dead. He appeared to many of his disciples before ascending to heaven, and he now sits at the right hand of God, very much alive, and interceding on our behalf.

Sin carries a hefty price tag and someone had to pay for it. Jesus was the only one who fit the bill. He lived a perfect sinless life, which made him the only acceptable sacrifice for sin. He died once and for all, and for all. He gave his life to free us from sin, shame, and all the power of the enemy.

And because he died and rose again, we have this promise: "Everyone who calls on the name of the Lord will be saved."[13] *Everyone.* What a wonderful promise! He's already done the hard work. We need only to believe in him, and in what he did on the cross, to receive forgiveness for our sins.

He is our intercessor, our representative, and our friend. In John 14:6, Jesus said, "I am the way, the truth, and the life. No one comes to the Father except through Me" (NKJV). There is no other way to get to heaven. There is no other way to get to the Father. Jesus is the only way. Christ bridges the gap!

10. Matt 27:46 NKJV.
11. Luke 23:46 NKJV.
12. John 19:30 NKJV.
13. Rom 10:13 NIV.

Jesus: The Lamb of God

For scarcely for a righteous man will one die; yet perhaps for a good man someone would even dare to die. But God demonstrates His own love toward us, in that while we were still sinners, Christ died for us.[14]

---

14. Rom 5:7–8 NKJV.

— CHAPTER 7 —

Satan: The Enemy of Our Souls

DESPITE WHERE YOU'RE FROM or what you believe, you've heard of him in one form or another. He may have been called Satan, the devil, Lucifer, or something else, but no matter which name you use, they all have one common theme—bad news. The name Satan means "adversary" or "enemy."[1] Simply put, what the Joker is to Batman, Satan is to God.

He is the enemy of God and opposes anything connected with him, including us. The devil is a liar and a deceiver. He's the meanest of the mean and the lowest of the low. He's pure evil. But, surprisingly, he wasn't always that way. So, what happened? Where did he come from, and what does he want?

Well, he came from God. Yes, believe it or not, Satan, or Lucifer as he was called back then, was created by God, and was indeed a beautiful creature. But he wasn't just any old creature. He was an angelic being. I suppose he was sort of a "big shot" in heaven, as most believe he was the highest-ranking cherub. Cherubs are a class of supernatural beings who serve in the presence of God.[2]

Most scholars believe and agree that it's Lucifer mentioned in the book of Ezekiel 28, described as being the seal of perfection. He was full of wisdom and perfect in beauty. His very name meant

---

1. Bryant, *Zondervan Compact Bible Dictionary*, 526.
2. Kohlenberger, *NIV Exhaustive Bible Concordance*, 1417.

"light-bearer." He was covered with precious stones, including the diamond, the sapphire, the emerald, and gold, and his ways were perfect from the start.[3] Some believe he was even in charge of musical worship in heaven. Indeed, he must have been something to look at. However, despite the beauty and authority he possessed, he still wasn't satisfied. These things weren't enough for this now-fallen angel. He wanted more—much more.

The Fall of Lucifer

So, how did he become so mean and evil? Well, the short answer is pride—one of what we refer to as "the seven deadly sins." Pride, which is basically the worship of one's own self and achievements, is widely considered the worst sin. But, why is it the worst sin?" Well, for starters, it's the sin the devil committed, so that automatically shoots it to the top of the list.

That should really close this Q & A; but to go a little further, pride is said to be the root cause of nearly every other sin. Let's just throw out some examples, shall we? Consider murder, theft, and envy. In general, what might be the root cause of these sins? What could be the true motive behind them? Why would one commit such crimes against another human being? Yep, you guessed it. It's P-R-I-D-E. Pride can lead us to do abnormal things to satisfy our selfish egos.

So, the more Lucifer considered his amazing beauty and splendor, the more prideful he became. He began to think more of himself than what he was, which was simply a created being. He was so lifted up with pride, and had his head so far in the clouds, that he wanted to be in the place of God. Apparently, he thought he was better than the one who created him; but he found out he wasn't even close.

After successfully convincing a third of the angels to join his futile attempt to oust God, he and those who foolishly sided with him were expelled from heaven, never to return. Thus, Lucifer

---

3. Ezek 28:11–17 NKJV.

became Satan. What a way to fall, right? And what a great fall it must have been. Here is the truth: whether in heaven or on earth, any place beneath or in between, there is none who can stand against the Everlasting God—none.

Does Satan Have Influence Today?

Don't be fooled. Satan has power on earth. He works around the clock looking for any opportunity to wreak havoc and destruction in our lives. The fact is, he can have a major influence on the everyday choices we make, such as whether to be selfish or to give, whether to lie or tell the truth, and whether to love or to hate.

You may imagine a cartoon devil with a pitchfork, sitting on someone's shoulder, while opposing an identically sized angel on the opposite shoulder. The angel tries to persuade the person to do right, while the devil prompts them to consider all the ways they can selfishly benefit from doing wrong. After going back and forth pleading their cases, they poof into little clouds and disappear. The person is then left to make a difficult moral decision.

Although not as cute as the cartoon devil, Satan sweetly whispers lies to us so we'll sin against God. Not only that, but if he successfully convinces us to sin, he likes to make us feel guilty about it later. He hopes we'll feel too unworthy to approach God for forgiveness, so that we'll drift further from him, and further into sin. Satan knows that if we continue in willful sin, the end for us is death. He has no mercy for us and no concern for our well-being.

I mean, think about it. If you were facing a definite and impending doom, how would you react? And what if lying on top of that huge mound of negativity was the fact that you had to witness others—whom you consider lesser than yourself—freely receiving what you once enjoyed, but never will again? How would you feel? What incentive would you have to keep with your moral standards? What reason would you have to be kind and to care for others?

Satan: The Enemy of Our Souls

Well, the devil is angry. I take that back—he is absolutely furious. He's not sitting quietly on the sidelines watching things play out, but he's going down kicking and screaming. He hates us because we get to enjoy fellowship with God, both on earth and, even more so, when we get to heaven. He is the sorest of all losers. He hates God and he knows how much God loves us; therefore, his plan is to get back at God by completely destroying us—both body and soul.

He doesn't want us to have a relationship with the Lord, and he doesn't want us to experience heaven. He knows he's doomed for eternity, and he's looking to take along as many of us as possible. Sadly, he's increasing his soul count daily. But, how is he accomplishing this? If Satan is so horrible, how in the world does he even appeal to us? I'll tell you how. He does it with lies, deceit, and temptation.

Just as he tempted Eve in the garden, he continues to deceive us today. He dresses up sin to make it look pretty, desirable, and appealing, so that we'll want to take a huge bite. The devil lies to us and says the crimes we commit against God won't lead to consequences. He says, "A little bit of this or a little bit of that won't hurt." But Satan is the father of lies.[4] His sole mission, and his only intent, is to steal, to kill, and destroy.[5] He wants to steal our joy, peace, and happiness; he looks to kill our hope, faith, and mortal bodies; and he's seeking the destruction of our souls.

Now, let's get real for a moment. Satan had the guts to try and tempt Jesus,[6] so we're not excluded from his path of destruction. Also, he persuaded a third of the angels to rebel against God, so how much more are we subject to believe his lies and fall for his deception? How are we to successfully go against such a devious and compelling power? The answer is, we don't. At least not alone.

There is a spiritual war going on in the background of our lives. However, this battle is not ours, but it belongs to the Lord. We just happen to be in the middle of it. Nevertheless, we have a

---

4. John 8:44.
5. John 10:10.
6. Matt 4:1–11.

For the Potential Christian

choice to make. We must pick a side. If we want to follow Satan and live a life that embraces sin, we will perish. But if we choose to trust Jesus, he will give us power to stand against this crafty enemy. If we're on the Lord's side, we're already victorious because we're on the winning team. That's because God doesn't lose—ever.

> The thief does not come except to steal, and to kill, and to destroy. I have come that they may have life, and that they may have it more abundantly.[7]

---

7. John 10:10 NKJV.

— Chapter 8 —

Hell: Punishment for the Wicked

Some people don't believe hell exists. They claim it's made up, a myth, or simply a state of mind. Others suggest it's a concept created to control people with fear. They say hell is an attempt to coerce us into following the laws of society, or the rules of a specific religion. There are even Christians who don't believe in hell. Each group or individual has their own reasoning, but a common argument is that they believe God is too loving and too kind to send anyone to a place like hell, to be tormented forever.

Then, some believe in hell but refuse to talk about it. They say it convinces people to steer clear of God. Their theory is that talking about hell will make people believe God is cruel, so they'll want nothing to do with him. Others think mentioning hell may cause a person to accept Christ, but only out of fear, making the person's salvation ungenuine.

Hell is indeed a scary place, however, Jesus didn't teach, and we don't preach, on hell to frighten unbelievers into the kingdom of heaven. Instead, it's done out of love, as we want those without this knowledge to be informed. It's no different than when our parents, grandparents, teachers, etc. warned us about the consequences of disobeying the law. They didn't want us to end up in jail or worse.

In the same way, Jesus doesn't want anyone to end up in that horrible place called hell—especially due to ignorance. However, he doesn't want us to come to him because we're afraid, but because we understand how much he loves us. He loved us so much that he died so we wouldn't have to go to hell. That's the real message. He wants a love relationship with us, and not one based on fear.

Besides, Jesus said those who love him will keep his commandments. If you don't love him, you won't follow his teachings, and if you don't follow his teachings, you are not his true follower. Has anyone ever scared you into loving them? Has anyone ever forced your affection with fear? Experience and common sense tell us that fear alone cannot cause a person to truly love and obey anyone. It's simply not enough. Fear of hell does not make disciples, but the love of Christ does. One cannot sincerely serve God because fear forces them, but they can truly serve the Lord when love persuades them.

Why Hell?

Hell is a real place and, unfortunately, people go there every day—good people, bad people, and even in-between people. There are many who try to reason it away, but there is plenty of biblical evidence to support the reality of hell. In fact, Jesus speaks a lot about it in the Bible, so we can assume it's a pretty important matter.

And why wouldn't it be? It's literally a matter of life and death. Nevertheless, we won't spend much time on it because I don't plan to go there and neither should you. So, what do we know about it? Well, Jesus describes hell on multiple occasions as being a place of "outer darkness" where there will be "weeping and gnashing of teeth."[1] It will be a place of agonizing torment and sorrow.

> The Son of Man will send his angels, and they will remove from his Kingdom everything that causes sin and all who do evil. And the angels will throw them into the fiery furnace, where there will be weeping and gnashing of teeth.[2]

---

1. Matt 8:12.
2. Matt 13:41–42 NLT.

Hell: Punishment for the Wicked

God is not cruel or hateful, as some make him out to be. Their lack of understanding paints a false picture of him in their minds, and that's the only way they choose to see him. They don't try to understand who he really is. But God sent his only Son in the world to suffer and die for us. That's something that could have only been done out of love. However, as we discussed previously, God hates sin; and because of his perfect nature, he cannot allow it to go unpunished. Hell is the place prepared for that punishment.

An unregenerate soul, that is, a soul that has rejected Jesus Christ, will not enter a righteous heaven. Unless a person is born again (which we'll discuss in a later chapter), he or she cannot enter the kingdom of God.[3] Our souls were made to last forever. We don't simply die then cease to exist. When our physical bodies expire, our souls must go somewhere, and only two places will last for the duration of eternity. If heaven is not the soul's final destination, there's only one other place it can go—that place of everlasting punishment.

What Is Hell Like?

Just like heaven, many people claim they've visited hell. While I don't dispute anyone's experience, clearly everyone isn't telling the truth. Some may sincerely believe they've been there, but in truth they were only dreaming. Several times I've awakened myself and couldn't determine whether something was or wasn't a dream. Therefore, the only reliable information we can use to see what hell is like is in the Word of God.

The book of Luke tells the story of a rich man who lived well on earth, and another man, Lazarus, who was a poor beggar. Both men died and the selfish rich man went to hell, while Lazarus was taken by angels to "Abraham's bosom," which is a symbol of blessedness after death.[4] The rest of the story goes like this:

---

3. John 3:3.
4. Bryant, *Zondervan Compact Bible Dictionary*, 16.

> "In Hades, where he was in torment, he looked up and saw Abraham far away, with Lazarus by his side. So he called to him, 'Father Abraham, have pity on me and send Lazarus to dip the tip of his finger in water and cool my tongue, because I am in agony in this fire.' But Abraham replied, 'Son, remember that in your lifetime you received your good things, while Lazarus received bad things, but now he is comforted here and you are in agony. And besides all this, between us and you a great chasm has been set in place, so that those who want to go from here to you cannot, nor can anyone cross over from there to us.' He answered, 'Then I beg you, father, send Lazarus to my family, for I have five brothers. Let him warn them, so that they will not also come to this place of torment.'"[5]

We can conclude several things from the above Scripture. First, hell is a place of agony and torment. Second, there's no way to jump a fence to get from hell to heaven. Like my mother used to say, "You're stuck like Chuck." Third, it's a place where you wouldn't want your family, friends, or even your worst enemy to end up. It's just that bad. Finally, we can see that hell is a place none of us would want to be.

The Bible says it will be a place of great suffering. It's described as a furnace of fire[6] whose residents will be forever separated from God.[7] Some scholars believe hell, or Hades, is a place where the wicked go after death to await final judgment. They believe it's a holding place on the way to their final destination, which is the lake of fire. Revelation tells us that everyone whose name is not found in the Book of Life will be cast into a lake of fire, where there will be torment both day and night.[8] Interestingly, the lake of fire wasn't created for human beings, but was instead prepared for Satan and his crew.[9] However, anyone who chooses to follow their

---

5. Luke 16:23–28 NIV.
6. Matt 13:50.
7. 2 Thess 1:7–9.
8. Rev 20:15.
9. Matt 25:41.

Hell: Punishment for the Wicked

evil ways will also be required to follow them into the lake of fire on the day of judgment.

Hell is a place to avoid at all costs. It is nothing to be desired and there's nothing good about it. Some create long debates to argue the specifics of hell. But regardless of the details, disputes, and theological arguments, the essential point is that hell is a place where the sweet presence of God is not, yet the wrath of God is. Thankfully, because of his grace and mercy, the Lord has established a way for us to escape it.

> He will punish those who do not know God and do not obey the gospel of our Lord Jesus. They will be punished with everlasting destruction and shut out from the presence of the Lord and from the glory of his might.[10]

---

10. 2 Thess 1:8–9 NIV.

— Chapter 9 —

Heaven: The Reward of the Righteous

"This world is not my home." More than likely you've heard someone say that before. You may or may not have known what they meant by it. Basically, it means that although we currently live in the world, we are only passing through. We are sojourners—simply strangers in a foreign land. We aren't meant to live here forever because a Christian's true citizenship is in heaven.[1]

You see, when one becomes a Christian, he or she becomes a brand-new person. At that point, all the old things pass away, and everything about them becomes new.[2] This includes their home. Although believers are left here temporarily as ambassadors for Christ and are subject to laws of the land, we no longer follow popular culture and practices that may violate the laws of heaven. We abandon the temporary pleasures that once ruled our lives, and instead we fix our eyes above, as our souls long to be with our Father in our new home—heaven.

But surprisingly, the Bible doesn't give a lot of information about the place. Personally, I think it's because God wants us to be eager to get there and find out more for ourselves; but that's just my theory. I believe heaven is a place so extraordinary that our minds can't begin to accurately imagine it. However, through

1. Phil 3:20.
2. 2 Cor 5:17.

certain passages of Scripture, we're offered a small glimpse—a very brief, yet sweet taste of heaven—which we can now savor until the day we experience it in its completeness.

What Will Heaven Be Like?

Almost everyone likes to imagine heaven. We ponder what it will look like, who will be there, what we will do all day, and more. Unfortunately, our curiosity won't be completely satisfied until we cross that glorious threshold. But the book of Revelation gives us an idea of what heaven will be like:

> Then the angel showed me a river with the water of life, clear as crystal, flowing from the throne of God and of the Lamb. It flowed down the center of the main street. On each side of the river grew a tree of life, bearing twelve crops of fruit, with a fresh crop each month. The leaves were used for medicine to heal the nations.
> No longer will there be a curse upon anything. For the throne of God and of the Lamb will be there, and his servants will worship him. And they will see his face, and his name will be written on their foreheads. And there will be no night there—no need for lamps or sun—for the Lord God will shine on them. And they will reign forever and ever.[3]

Wow! Did you read that too? The Bible says that in heaven there will be rivers as clear as crystal, no more curses, and we won't have need for the sun because the Lord God will shine on us and be our light. That means no more sweltering heat and no more sunburns to deal with. If you've ever lived in Texas, trust me, that's good news. And how many times have you stayed up all night crying about this or worrying about that? Well, I have more good news for you. The Bible says God will wipe away all tears.[4]

There will be no more death, sorrow, or crying in heaven. That means no more turning on the news and hearing of

3. Rev 22:1–5 NLT.
4. Rev 21:4.

numerous fatalities resulting from murder, wrecks, disease, and carelessness. There will be no more crying over the death of loved ones; in fact, there will be no concern over death at all because it will be obsolete.

Poverty and hunger will be an issue no longer, as the wealthy man will dwell with the poor man. There are no social or financial statuses in heaven, and nothing to create division. There will be no more rape and no more heartache; no more fighting and no more loneliness. And pain? Forget about it! There will be no more pain. It will be paradise, and all of our troubles in this world will be over. I don't know about you, but I get excited just thinking about it!

Billy Graham once suggested that "Heaven will be what we have always longed for. It will be the new social order that men dream of. All the things that have made earth unlovely and tragic will be absent in Heaven. There will be no night, no death, no disease, no sorrow, no tears, no ignorance, no disappointment, no war. It will be filled with happiness, worship, love, and perfection."[5]

Martin Luther, one of the most influential figures in the history of Christianity, once stated, "I would not give one moment of heaven for all the joy and riches of the world, even if it lasted for thousands and thousands of years."[6] I second that statement. A moment in heaven with Jesus—even one that's very brief—isn't worth giving up for any amount of treasure, or any number of lifetimes on earth. Every moment we spend there will be priceless.

Hope in the Resurrection

Our hope in the afterlife is the reason we can have peace in a chaotic world. We trust that something better awaits us. Given all the pain and suffering we're exposed to, if we put our faith in this world only, we would be miserable creatures. What real joy can one have knowing they're living for this life alone? What peace do

---

5. BGEA staff, "What Will Heaven Be Like?"
6. Quoted from Quotes.net. https://www.quotes.net/quote/15317.

Heaven: The Reward of the Righteous

we have if we believe that when we shut our eyes for the last time and take our final breath there will be nothing else after?

What if everything we are simply ends when we die? All the relationships we've built won't matter since there'd be no chance to see those people again. What would have been the purpose of living? But we believe that when we die is when our lives truly begin. We believe that just as Jesus was raised to life, we too will be raised to life in the resurrection. You may ask, "What is the resurrection?" Well, before he went to heaven, Jesus revealed to his disciples that in his Father's house there are many rooms. He said he was going to prepare a place for them, and that he would come back to get them so they could be where he is.[7] This promise of heaven is also true for those who believe in Christ today.

The first time Jesus came to earth, he came to die for our sins. I guess you could say he cleared the path to heaven by removing the obstacles that were in our way. Sin stood in our way to eternal life, but Jesus removed it when he died on the cross. Now, when he comes the second time, he's not leaving us behind this go-round. He's taking all those who are prepared back to heaven with him—all those who have accepted his gift of salvation.

In the resurrection, the Lord will come from heaven with a shout and with the trumpet of God. All those who died believing in him will rise first. Then, those who are still alive and have put their faith in Christ will be caught up together with them in the clouds. They will meet the Lord in the air, and will be with him forever.[8] When he comes back for his children—the true believers—the Bible says we will be changed.

We will have incorruptible bodies that are not subject to death, pain, or disease. We don't know what these bodies will look like, but what we know is that we'll be like Jesus; for we will see him as he is.[9] I believe heaven is an awesome and wonderful place, filled with joy, love, and peace. However, the best thing about it is that we'll finally be where the Lord is, and we'll get to see his face.

7. John 14:2–3.
8. 1 Thess 4:14–18.
9. 1 John:3:2.

For the Potential Christian

That's what heaven truly is. That's what it's all about. It's a place where we'll get to spend eternity with our Creator and worship him endlessly—all of us who are his children, at home with our Father forever.

> "Again, the kingdom of heaven is like a merchant seeking beautiful pearls, who, when he had found one pearl of great price, went and sold all that he had and bought it."[10]

---

10. Matt 13:45-46 NKJV.

— *Chapter 10* —

What Does It Mean to Repent?

On the day of Pentecost, as described in the book of Acts, Jesus's disciples were gathered in one place, in Jerusalem. Jesus had been crucified, buried, and resurrected, and he'd already ascended to heaven. Before he left, he promised them they would soon be baptized with the Holy Spirit, at which time they would receive power from on high. And so, it happened that as they all sat together in one place a sound came from heaven as of a rushing mighty wind, and it filled the entire house. They were all filled with the Holy Ghost, and began speaking in unlearned languages, as the Spirit enabled them to do so.

There were people from every nation dwelling in Jerusalem, and when they heard the noise, a large crowd came together and was confused. They were perplexed because each heard the disciples speaking to them in their native language. This was puzzling to them because they knew the disciples, who were Galilean, shouldn't have been able to speak these languages, yet somehow they spoke them fluently.

Everyone understood the disciples in their own language, but they all heard them speaking the same thing. They were proclaiming the wonderful things of God. Some were amazed and others were in doubt. In search of answers, they asked one another, "What does this mean?" Some even accused the disciples of being drunk, even though it was only 9 o'clock in the morning. That's when Peter, also known as Cephas, stood up and addressed the crowd.

Peter began by saying that the men weren't drunk, but what they were witnessing was the work of the Holy Spirit, which was previously spoken of by the prophet Joel. He went on to tell them that God clearly showed his approval of Jesus by the signs, miracles, and wonders that he had done through him, and that Jesus was given to them to die because it was part of God's plan.

Then, Peter accused the crowd. He said that with the help of wicked men they crucified and killed Jesus of Nazareth, but that God had raised him from the dead. He declared that he and the other disciples were witnesses to his resurrection. The apostle ended his message by telling them that "God has made this Jesus, whom you crucified, both Lord and Christ."[1]

When the multitude heard this, the Bible says they were "pricked in their heart"[2] or, as some translations say, they were "cut to the heart" (NKJV), meaning they were overcome with grief because of what they had done. This was a natural reaction to realizing they'd killed the very person who came to save them. They asked Peter and the other disciples, "Men and brothers, what shall we do?" Peter answered them and said, "Repent, and be baptized every one of you in the name of Jesus Christ for the remission of sins, and ye shall receive the gift of the Holy Ghost."[3]

Basically, if they wanted forgiveness of their sins, the first thing they needed to do was repent. Repentance is an important part of the salvation process, but it's easily misunderstood. Although some misunderstandings in life can be harmless, a misunderstanding about repentance can be a hindrance to salvation, so it's important to correctly understand it. So, let's take a look at repentance, shall we?

---

1. Acts 2:36 NKJV.
2. Acts 2:37 KJV.
3. Acts 2:37–38 KJV.

What Does It Mean to Repent?

Derek Prince, an outstanding Bible teacher while on earth, once said that repentance is not an emotion, but a decision.[4] In other words, repentance doesn't mean one walks toward the altar with tears streaming so heavy they nearly drown the church, but with no real intention of changing. Repentance is not a temporary, here-today–gone-tomorrow feeling. In fact, it's not a feeling at all. It involves making a conscious decision to turn from the wrong direction to the right one.[5]

Repentance means to have a "change of mind"[6] and it involves a turning away from sin.[7] It can also mean "to feel regret" or "remorse."[8] Some debate the biblical meaning of the word—whether it means to change one's mind or to turn away from sin—but if we look at the bigger picture, we can see it all goes hand in hand. You see, when we change our mind about something, the result is a change in our actions. Essentially, what we're doing is deciding to turn away from one thing to turn toward something else. Our actions are the visible results of those decisions.

Consider the vehicle you use each day. The steering wheel controls the entire hunk of metal. It's sort of like the control center, or the brain. It's similar to our minds being that it gives the orders and directs the rest of the machine. It cannot turn left or right without the vehicle's body following in agreement, and if we're truly convinced of a thing, neither is it possible for our minds and our actions to proceed in opposite directions. What we do is the result of what we think and believe. Just as we change direction when the GPS tells us we're going the wrong way, so do we turn and follow a new road when our minds redirect our thinking.

---

4. Prince, "Repentance."
5. Prince, "Repentance."
6. Kohlenberger, *NIV Exhaustive Bible Concordance*, 948.
7. Bryant, *Zondervan Compact Bible Dictionary*, 495.
8. *Merriam-Webster.com Dictionary*, "repent," https://www.merriam-webster.com/dictionary/repent.

So, when the people in Jerusalem understood they had killed the Messiah, they wanted to know how to make things right. The first thing Peter answered and said to them was, "Repent," or change your minds. In other words, recognize that you're going the wrong way and turn around. The Bible says those who believed Peter's words were baptized, added to the church, and continued in the apostles' teachings. Because they changed their minds, their actions followed in the same direction. So, here's how this comes together for us.

When we change our minds about sin and turn from unbelief to belief, we agree that Jesus is who he says he is, and that he can do what he says he can do. We believe he is the Savior of the world, he can save us from our sins, and he is the only way to eternal life. This new way of thinking prompts us to turn from a life of darkness toward his marvelous light. Once we receive Jesus's offer of forgiveness, we begin connecting with him on an intimate level. We start to learn of his character, and as we do we feel remorse as we realize we've transgressed, or sinned, against a loving and holy God.

We develop a sheer hatred for the sin we once loved, and we decide to have nothing more to do with it. And why should we? After all, our Savior suffered a horrible death because of it. Does a mother who's lost her child to drunk driving not have a strong hatred toward the very idea of one driving while intoxicated? Does she not become a voice that rises up against it? So it is also with the one who has understood that because of our sin, Jesus, the one we love, was painfully crucified and killed. Sin becomes the enemy.

Therefore, it's safe to say that, as it pertains to Christianity, to repent means to change one's mind and believe in Christ, but a natural result of that change of mind is to turn away from sin. When our mind switches up its course, everything else follows suit. It's like a chain reaction. A changed mind results in a changed heart, which leads to a change in actions, and ultimately a changed life. True repentance consists of all of these elements and not just one. It's a complete package.

What Does It Mean to Repent?

Why Do We Need to Repent?

When we hear the gospel, we're enlightened. However, we're also faced with the reality that we're terribly flawed in comparison to God. It's like we're in a dark interrogation room with a spotlight shining from above, fixated on all our flaws and failures. There's nowhere to hide from the light. In the light, we're forced to see who we really are and how wrong we've been about believing we're a "good person." When we're exposed to God's truth, God's truth exposes us. Nevertheless, this isn't a bad thing. Realizing how much we fall short shows us we're in pretty bad shape and that we're in desperate need of a Savior.

When we accept this reality, it leads us to turn to Jesus, who himself said he will reject no one who comes to him.[9] Repentance is important because it opens the door to salvation. If we don't change our mind about who Jesus is, then we can't place our faith in him. If we can't place our faith in him, then we can't be saved. If we die unsaved, then heaven will not be our home. It's just that simple.

If we don't believe there's a problem, there's no need to search for an answer, and if we don't think we need saving, we won't look for a Savior. A change of mind must take place. Our thoughts about who we are, who Jesus is, and what he's done must change. Very simply, we need to repent because if we don't, we will perish in our sins. The first message Jesus preached was one that called for repentance.[10] There are no exceptions. God commands every one, everywhere, to repent.[11]

How Do We Repent?

No one can come to Jesus unless the Father first draws them to him.[12] Jesus made this clear. God draws us to him with love and kindness, and he draws whom he wills, in his time, and in his way.

9. John 6:37.
10. Matt 4:17.
11. Acts 17:30.
12. John 6:44.

For the Potential Christian

It's an act of his divine mercy. It's not a result of anything we are, anything we have, or anything we've done. It is a gift. This drawing can come in many forms.

One might begin searching for the meaning of life, or they may begin having thoughts about God. There could be a chronic emptiness in the soul that the person desperately seeks to fill, or some tragic event may occur that causes them to ask questions about life, death, and eternity. It may happen in various ways, but as God begins to lay hold of our hearts, we become aware of our sinful state and we become sorrowful.

The Bible tells us that godly sorrow produces repentance that leads to salvation.[13] When we hear the gospel and believe it, we feel true regret and sorrow over the fact that we've sinned against God. Just like those who put Jesus to death, we are cut to the heart. We agree that God's Word is true, and that, as it states, we are sinners. Then, we ask the question, "What can I do about it?" The answer is repent.

So, what does this look like? When you feel God's loving hand tugging at the strings of your heart, don't turn away. If you hear a whisper in your spirit, urging you to do what's right, don't ignore that voice. When you feel guilt over your sin—about the things you know are wrong—don't shrug it off and pretend it's okay. Make the decision to turn from sin and to follow God, and the Holy Spirit will help you do it.

God alone draws people to himself. Therefore, when he stretches his hand toward you, reach out and forcefully grab it. Don't let stubbornness, unbelief, or anything else stand in your way. Change your mind about Jesus Christ. I thank God with all my soul because I'm confident that if you feel even the tiniest prick in your heart, then it means this drawing is already taking place in your life.

---

13. 2 Cor 7:10.

What Does It Mean to Repent?

True Repentance vs. False Repentance

Now, I have a serious question for you. What is your motive for seeking God? Is it because you're truly sorry for your sins, or is it because you fear hell? In other words, is it because you're afraid of the consequences, or do you desire to do what's right? I once heard a sermon by Charles Spurgeon, a wise preacher from the 1800s, where he suggested that in the case of some who confess Christ, if the consequence of hellfire were taken away, they would run back to their sinful habits.

This behavior does not signify true repentance. Instead, it's a characteristic of false repentance, which is temporary, meaning it would be a matter of time before the person returns to their old ways—however long it takes for the flame of fear to cool off. Although sin is enjoyable for a moment, when we realize how it harms our overall well-being—our minds, bodies, and souls—we are motivated to turn away from it. More importantly, when we understand how it breaks the heart of God, we make a commitment to forsake it.

True repentance means you are repulsed by your sin. Once you step away from it, you don't look back and desire to pick up where you left off. On the contrary, you try your best to push the very thought of it out of your mind. Instead of those old sinful habits, you now want to do what's right and pleasing in God's sight. It becomes your mission to rid yourself of every speck and every stench of sin in your life. Of course, there will be times when you fail, but those times should be exceptions and not the norm.

It's important to also mention, and to make very clear, that we can't truly turn from sin until we receive salvation. Before conversion, we don't have the power to do so. That kind of power only comes from the Holy Spirit, which is given to those who willfully surrender their lives to Christ. We can get caught up thinking we need to change before we're considered good enough to approach Jesus, but the truth is, we will never be good enough.

There is nothing we can do to make us acceptable to the Lord. We are made righteous through him only, and our self-righteousness is like filthy rags to God.[14] Our own efforts are useless. That's why I stated in the beginning that a misunderstanding about repentance can be a hindrance to our salvation. Since we can't change on our own, if we continue to try, we're likely to give up and never come to Jesus. We'll lose hope when we continue to fail. Though we could try a thousand times, it is not possible to change ourselves. We need the power of God.

Now friend, let me level with you for a moment. Some things, in the beginning, might be a struggle to let go of. That's because our "flesh"—which is what we call our "sin nature"—won't allow us to let sin go without a fight. However, with the power of God, through his Holy Spirit, we win those fights. If we don't give in, we win. The letter of James says in verse 4:7 that if we submit ourselves to God and resist the devil, then the devil will flee from us. That's right. All true believers are given power to make Satan flee! But we have to both submit to one and resist the other as the Scripture indicates.

As we continue to resist temptation, it becomes easier for us to turn our back on sin and to keep it turned. Whereas now those sinful urges may be as a roaring lion in your ear, they will eventually sound like tiny annoying bugs that require little effort to squash. Now, listen to this closely: no matter what some believe or practice, willful and habitual sin have no place in the life of a believer. True repentance results in a changed life. The changes may be small and gradual at first, but a change nonetheless.

And this thing I assure you: whatever it is you're turning away from, and whatever it is you're giving up, it can't possibly compare to the great things God has in store for you, and the wonderful plans he has for your life. Aren't you tired of trying it your way? Are your plans just not working out? Well, friend, it's time to try Jesus. Repent! For the kingdom of heaven is at hand.

> Now after that John was put in prison, Jesus came into Galilee, preaching the gospel of the kingdom of God, And saying, The time is fulfilled, and the kingdom of God is at hand: repent ye, and believe the gospel.[15]

14. Isa 64:6.
15. Mark 1:14–15 KJV.

— CHAPTER 11 —

What Is Salvation?

BEFORE WE TURN TO Jesus for salvation, incriminating evidence is piled against us, and ironically the only way we can avoid a death sentence is to plead guilty. Yes, I know it sounds backwards; but we have to throw ourselves down at the foot of Christ and admit before the Righteous Judge that we are guilty of sin. However, once we make our admission of guilt, we're not condemned as in a human court; instead of losing our case, we find something: mercy—God's mercy.

Now, this won't happen in real life, but for a moment picture yourself in a courtroom. I'll set the scene for you. Imagine you're on trial for committing a horrible crime. You've just pleaded guilty, and you're on pins and needles as you await your final sentencing. All kinds of thoughts are running through your brain. Just thinking of the what-ifs has your mind feeling dizzy. You try to remain hopeful, but you keep imagining ill-fated scenarios.

Then, you bow your head to pray. You're still not sure if there is a God, but just in case he exists you promise him if he gets you out of this, you'll turn your whole life around. Suddenly, the judge re-enters the room. Your thoughts come to an abrupt end. Okay—this is it. Everyone is now standing, and the entire room is as silent as a church before a prayer. Alright. Here it comes.

The next few moments feel like forever. You hold your breath as the judge begins to speak, and after you hear his words you

For the Potential Christian

develop a lump in the middle of your throat. How could this be? Your worst fear has come true. The judge has just sentenced you to life in prison, and it feels as if you can't breathe. Air! You need air! Your heart drops into your stomach, and the room begins to spin. The reality starts to hit you square in the face: your life is over, and there's nothing you can do about it. You would make it right if you could, but there's no way to go back and fix it.

Then, suddenly, in the midst of the commotion, you see a man calmly walking toward the judge. Your weary eyes begin to follow him as he slowly approaches the bench. He speaks to the judge for several moments, then hurriedly walks away. Suddenly, the judge looks up, bangs his gavel, and calls for order in the courtroom. Once things calm down, he looks at you dead in the eye and says, "Well, it looks like you're free to go. Someone agreed to take your punishment. They agreed to take your place. All the charges have been dropped. You are free to go in peace."

How would you feel in that moment? There would be no words to describe it, right? The only thing you have to do is accept the fact that someone you didn't know has taken the fall for a crime you undeniably committed, and you can walk out of that courtroom a free man or woman. How unbelievable is that? Somebody decided to give up *their* life so you could keep yours.

Sure, it's a stretch. But I wanted to give you a general understanding of how Jesus sacrificed his life for us. Christ took our place, and took the punishment for our sins. He satisfied God's judgment for the crimes we committed, by enduring God's wrath on the cross. He died so we could have eternal life, and also new life here on earth.

You see, when we are forgiven, not only does God remove the punishment from us, but he removes our sins from us as far as the east is from the west.[1] He remembers them no more.[2] There is no such thing as a "permanent record" with God once we give our lives to him. That's because, in his amazing grace, he wipes our slate clean. He gives us a brand-new life, and a brand-new start.

1. Ps 103:12.
2. Isa 43:25.

What Is Salvation?

We are spiritually cleansed by the purifying blood that Jesus shed on the cross for our sins. His blood covers us, and we are hidden beneath it. So, now when God looks at us, he doesn't see the filth of our sin, but he sees the precious blood of his Son; and since he no longer finds any evidence against us, he issues a brand-new verdict: *Not Guilty*.

What Does It Mean to Be Saved?

In my opinion, salvation is one of the simplest, yet most complex subjects to grasp. That's because God made it so simple that even a child can understand it, yet, being the natural overthinkers we are, we tend to complicate it. Nevertheless, any way you look at it, salvation should be the most important thing on the heart and mind of every human being. That's because where we spend eternity depends on whether or not we've received salvation through Jesus Christ. So, what is salvation, and what does it mean to be saved?

Let's start with a basic definition. Salvation means to be preserved or to be delivered from destruction, ruin, or harm. To be delivered also means to be rescued. So, what type of destruction or harm are we being rescued from? We're rescued from the consequences of sin, which includes the eternal destruction of our souls. God is angry with the wicked every day.[3] His wrath builds against all those who live a life of willful sin and reject Jesus Christ as their Lord and Savior.[4] Therefore, when we're saved, we no longer need to fear God's wrath.

> When you follow the desires of your sinful nature, the results are very clear: sexual immorality, impurity, lustful pleasures, idolatry, sorcery, hostility, quarreling, jealousy, outbursts of anger, selfish ambition, dissension, division, envy, drunkenness, wild parties, and other sins like these. Let me tell you again, as I have before, that anyone living that sort of life will not inherit the Kingdom of God.[5]

3. Ps 7:11.
4. Rom 2:5.
5. Gal 5:19–21 NLT.

For the Potential Christian

No one practicing such sins as those stated above will inherit the Kingdom of God—God's Word, not mine. But, when we're saved, we're rescued from the clutches of darkness, which prevent us from living holy and pleasing to the Lord. We are no longer slaves to sin as we're given power over temptation. We become free to live a righteous life, which is both commanded by God, and yields heavenly rewards.

How Are We Saved?

In the previous chapter, we discussed repentance, which means to change one's mind. If you recall, when we change our minds about Jesus, we turn from unbelief to belief in him. Repentance and belief are very closely related. They are so connected that they're commonly described as being "two sides of the same coin." Now, we'll look at the opposite side of that coin, which is belief—the chief ingredient in salvation.

In the book of Acts, we encounter two men named Paul and Silas. While in a place called Philippi, these men of God were beaten and thrown into prison because they ruffled the feathers of certain slave owners.[6] At midnight, while in prison, Paul and Silas began to pray and sing songs to God while the other prisoners listened. Suddenly, there was a great earthquake, and the ground of the prison began to shake. All the prison doors flung open, and every prisoner's chains were loosed. Let's take a look at what happens next.

> And the keeper of the prison, awaking from sleep and seeing the prison doors open, supposing the prisoners had fled, drew his sword and was about to kill himself. But Paul called with a loud voice, saying, "Do yourself no harm, for we are all here."
> Then he called for a light, ran in, and fell down trembling before Paul and Silas. And he brought them out and said, "Sirs, what must I do to be saved?"

---

6. Acts 16:16–24.

What Is Salvation?

> So they said, "Believe on the Lord Jesus Christ, and you will be saved, you and your household." Then they spoke the word of the Lord to him and to all who were in his house. And he took them the same hour of the night and washed their stripes. And immediately he and all his family were baptized.[7]

When the jailer asked Paul and Silas, "What must I do to be saved?," their response to him was to "believe on the Lord Jesus Christ, and you will be saved."

John 3:16, a well-known verse of Scripture, reads, "For God so loved the world, that he gave his only begotten Son, that whosoever believeth in him should not perish, but have everlasting life" (KJV). Again, there is that word "believe." Whoever believes in Jesus will not die an eternal death, but will have eternal life. Let's look at a couple more passages. Pay close attention to the relationship between belief and eternal life.

> "The Father loves his Son and has put everything into his hands. And anyone who believes in God's Son has eternal life. Anyone who doesn't obey the Son will never experience eternal life but remains under God's angry judgment."[8]

Now, read these words spoken by Jesus in John 5:24, and see if you can find the same correlation.

> "I tell you the truth, those who listen to my message and believe in God who sent me have eternal life. They will never be condemned for their sins, but they have already passed from death into life." (NLT)

So then, how are we are saved? We are saved by believing— that is, by believing that Jesus Christ is the Son of God, and that his blood was shed on the cross for the remission, or cancellation, of our sins. However, this is no common belief we're talking about here. Anyone can have a general belief in God. The letter of James tells us in verse 2:29 that even the demons believe and they tremble

---

7. Acts 16:27–33 NKJV.
8. John 3:35–36 NLT.

before him. They acknowledge God and believe he's all-powerful, but they can't be saved no matter how much they believe.

Many human beings act in the same manner. They have a general belief in God and profess to be Christians, but they haven't made Jesus Lord over their lives. Instead, they continue to live how they please, in blatant disregard of God's commandments. Now, in all fairness, some are honestly ignorant of what the Bible says. But, then again, that's because they haven't taken time to read it to find out what's in it. Therefore, ignorance is no excuse.

But, in the case of true salvation, when we hear the Gospel, or "Good News" of Jesus Christ, it opens the door for faith. When we accept what we hear as truth—that Jesus was crucified, buried, and resurrected—faith is invited in. This type of faith, known as "saving faith," moves us to take action. That action includes confessing Christ as Lord. This means we agree he is the Messiah, we acknowledge him before others, and we place him in complete control of our lives. It's making a commitment to follow his ways and to keep his commandments.

The Bible tells us that if we confess with our mouths that Jesus is Lord, and believe in our hearts that God raised him from the dead, we will be saved. When we believe, we are justified—which means God declares us to be righteous—and with our mouths we acknowledge that Jesus is in control. These are the things that save us.[9]

Sanctification

After we're saved, a transformation begins to take place. We have a renewed nature that is the result of being what Jesus refers to as "born again."[10] When we are spiritually reborn, our old life with its sinful habits dies, and we receive a new life that is now led by the Holy Spirit. When we accept Christ, the Holy Spirit, which is God's Spirit, comes to live inside of us.

---

9. Romans 10:9–10.
10. John 3:3.

What Is Salvation?

As the late great Bishop G. E. Patterson once stated, "Salvation is an inside job." This means the Holy Spirit changes us from the inside out. Our immoral desires no longer run the show because, as born-again believers, we have the power to resist temptation and live according to God's standards.

Our entire way of life is changed. The Spirit gradually transforms us to look more like Christ—both internally in our hearts and externally in our actions. He changes our thoughts, attitudes, and desires. Our lives become less about ourselves and more about pleasing God. As time passes, the sinful things we once thought were enjoyable no longer interest us. Instead, we find ourselves more attracted to the things of God, such as reading the Bible, fellowshipping with like-minded believers, and helping others.

However, we're not instantly changed with the twist of a wand like Cinderella. No fairy godmother will "bippity, boppity, boop" us into the picture-perfect saint. It takes time and effort, and the process isn't as beautiful. In fact, sometimes it's downright ugly. But the Christian way of life is one that must be learned. We are transformed by renewing our minds, which happens as we consistently study the Bible, pray, and spend time with the Lord. When we are born naturally, we must grow and learn. It is the same with our spiritual birth.

God's Word, coupled with the Holy Spirit, work to transform us daily. As a butterfly exits the cocoon, leaving behind its days as a caterpillar, so are we to leave our old selves behind and flourish in our new life, which is governed by Christ. It's a learning process; and as with anything new that must be learned, we'll make mistakes along the way; but the important thing is that we're *growing*. As these changes continue to take place on the inside, through a process called "sanctification," we'll begin to see the evidence of our changed life on the outside—and so will others.

> Therefore, if anyone is in Christ, he is a new creation; old things have passed away; behold, all things have become new.[11]

---

11. 2 Cor 5:17 NKJV.

— CHAPTER 12 —

Would You Like to Accept Jesus?

LET ME START BY saying you won't be saved by simply reading aloud or repeating back a dry "sinner's prayer"—not without being sincere, you won't. As I mentioned before, God knows the contents of our hearts and he knows if we're real or not. He knows if the words we're speaking on the outside match what we believe on the inside. You can't pull a fast one on him. Remember, he sees and knows everything. But, if you believe in Jesus Christ and that he died and rose again, and if you're sorry for your sin, salvation awaits you.

Don't wait until you're in front of a church altar. Remember, the Lord is present everywhere and he hears us wherever we are. In fact, when I gave my life to Christ, I was lying on the floor in front of my couch, watching a sermon on YouTube. I felt the Lord speaking to me through the message being preached, and at the end of the program the pastor gave an altar call for those who wanted to be saved.

I'd been in church many times before, and I'd heard the same typical invite, but this time it was different. This time, God wasn't only speaking to me, but I was actually listening. The pastor's message seemed to be specifically for me. He said what I needed to hear, when I needed to hear it. His words struck a match in my soul, a fire was kindled, and a flame began to burn. I wanted what he was offering; and until that moment I didn't believe I could have it, because in my mind it wasn't for me. But God showed me that wasn't true.

So, right there on the floor, with a softened heart and an eager spirit, I repeated each word the pastor spoke. As I did, tears flooded my eyes and overflowed on the banks of my cheeks. I couldn't have restrained them if I'd tried. It felt as if God were putting his arms around me and telling me everything was alright. I felt a sense of relief as a heavy weight was lifted off my chest. It felt like I had been—forgiven. Truly forgiven. I felt love in a way that I'd never experienced before. My heart filled with joy and I felt an overwhelming peace. In between tears, I repeated several times, "Lord, I've been looking for you all my life." And to have finally found him—the only thing I could do was rejoice.

That day, the course of my life changed forever and I have no regrets. I have no concern for the things left behind, and if I had to do it again, I would make the same choice. However, making that choice initially was a struggle. But it usually is. That's because letting go of our old way isn't easy. We want to hang on to the lifestyle we know best, rather than venture into unknown territory. And believe it or not, that's normal.

Matthew 19:16-22 tells a story about a rich young ruler who came up to Jesus and asked, "Good Master, what good thing shall I do, that I may have eternal life?" Jesus simply told him to keep the commandments, and to go and sell his possessions and give the money to the poor. He told him if he did these things, he could follow him, and have treasure in heaven. However, the young man walked away sorrowful because he had a lot of possessions and didn't want to give them up. He didn't want to change his lifestyle from having everything at his fingertips to depending on Jesus for his needs.

He possibly missed out on eternal life because he didn't want to part with his worldly goods, since they meant so much to him. He didn't realize that the earthly treasure he had couldn't compare to the heavenly treasure Jesus wanted to give him. Now, don't be mistaken. His wealth wasn't a bad thing in itself. But Jesus perceived that it meant more to him than he did, so he needed the

For the Potential Christian

young man to give it up. There can be nothing in our lives that we love more than the Lord, and nothing we worship in his place. At that point, it becomes an idol, which is dangerous, since it's sure to separate us from God. That's what happened with this young ruler.

What about you? Is there any good reason to not accept Jesus into your life right now? If not, and you're ready to surrender your life to Christ, wonderful! Feel free to skip to the final paragraph of this chapter and I'll be with you in a moment. But, if there *is* a reason that's keeping you from accepting him, what is that reason? Do you believe that he, she, or it is worth being separated from God for all eternity? Something so temporary that it could be here today and gone tomorrow?

It's better to sacrifice the morsel of pleasure this world offers than to miss out on the full feast of heaven. "For what shall it profit a man, if he shall gain the whole world, and lose his own soul? Or what shall a man give in exchange for his soul?"[1] If you truly believe this temporal object is worth more than eternal life, then my prayer is that God will open your eyes to see the truth before it's too late. My friend, there *is* a deadline and you don't want to miss it.

So, I'll ask you to do two things. Number one: Pray to the Lord with a sincere heart and ask him to make himself real to you. Ask him to open your eyes to the truth, so that it's clear and unmistakable. Number two: When he does, come on back here and skip to the final paragraph of this chapter, answer the altar call at church, or have a Christian friend pray with you to accept Jesus as your Lord and Savior. Whatever is the fastest way to get to him, *do it*. He loves you, and he's waiting.

Now, for you that are ready—God is so thrilled that you've decided to come home! And I am too! But first, let me make something clear to you so you're not misled. In your new life, every day won't be lollipops and gumdrops; but don't get discouraged. Your Heavenly Father will be there every step of the way, Jesus will never leave you nor forsake you, and the Holy Spirit will lead you and guide you in all things. Trust me—you've got a great team behind you.

1. Mark 8:36–37.

Would You Like to Accept Jesus?

Now, my brother, my sister, don't overanalyze any of this. Just simply take a moment and think about all God has done for you. Just remember that he woke you up this morning and allowed you to see another day that wasn't promised to you. Consider how he's kept you safe from danger you could see, and danger you couldn't see. He has graciously watched over you and spared your life for this day. He has preserved you for this very moment. Jesus loves you, friend. You know it. The evidence is in your heart right now as you feel him calling you. Don't push him away. Reach out for him. And when you're ready, I would like you to raise both hands as a sign of surrender to the Lord, and pray the below prayer—from the bottom of your heart, directly to God's heart.

> Lord, I'm sorry for everything I've done that was not pleasing to you. I believe that Jesus is the Son of God. I believe Jesus died for my sins on the cross and that God raised him from the dead three days later. Forgive me for my sins. Come into my heart. Come into my life. Change me and fill me with your precious Holy Spirit. Teach me, lead me, guide me—and help me live for you all the days of my life.
>
> In Jesus's name, amen.

Beloved—welcome to the family.

— CHAPTER 13 —

So, What Now?

WHAT DO YOU MEAN, "What now?" You rejoice! That's what! If you accepted Jesus as your Lord and Savior, you're now part of God's family. Welcome home! Your name is now written in the Lamb's Book of Life, and heaven is your final destination. Now, I wish I could tell you things get easier from here, but lying is one of the seven things God hates.

But I am going to share some truth with you. The truth is, it's time to square up. Why? Because it's going to be a fight; and at times it's going to get tough. But always remember you're not alone. You are on a winning team, so no matter which way the tables turn, you and I will come out victorious in the end, if we stay faithful to God.

However, every day won't be rough. A lot of days will be sweet. And although things may not get easier, in my opinion, they certainly do get better. The joy I've experienced since becoming a Christian is far greater than the trouble I've faced. I've come to accept that everyday won't be a "good" day; but I've come to understand that, with God on my side, I'll make it through every one of them. With his help, I can handle the trouble.

Now, before we part from each other, I want to share a few pieces of advice concerning your next steps. The first piece of advice is to find a group of Christian believers to fellowship with—as in people who believe in, and strive to live out, every word of God.

So, What Now?

People who not only talk the talk but also walk the walk. Don't try to go at it alone. Trust me. Fellowshipping with other saints who love the Lord is very important. Singing harmoniously to God, agreeing on his goodness, having someone explain something to you until you understand it, and swapping encouraging testimonies are things that cannot be neglected or substituted.

So, find a group of believers and meet with them regularly. It doesn't have to be in a church building, because the people of God are the "church"—not the building. It won't only benefit you, but you have something to contribute as well. Just like our human bodies need certain parts to function, the body of Christ can't properly function without all its parts—and you're a major part of it! Cheesy, I know. But it's true. As iron sharpens iron, so does one believer sharpen another.[1]

My next advice concerns baptism. Here's the advice: *get baptized!* Unfortunately, the subject of baptism is a very controversial topic within Christianity, which can cause a lot of confusion for new believers. There is much debate surrounding the issue of baptism. These debates include questions such as: Is baptism necessary for salvation? If so, when should baptism occur? How should we be baptized? Should would we be sprinkled with water, or should we be submerged in it? There are various scriptures and arguments to support some viewpoints, and if you would like, you can research them on your own. However, I won't waste your time or mine debating those issues here. But, I will share my personal experience, and what I believe based on God's Word and my own conviction.

I was baptized three years after converting to Christianity. You may ask, "Why did it take so long?" Well, it was due to a number of reasons, or better yet, excuses. Let's just say I decided to hold off for a while. But, as I was waiting, I began listening to some of the arguments against baptism, and began to think taking the plunge wasn't important. Well, I was wrong. I kept feeling this little nudge—this repetitive thought in my spirit that kept saying, "I need to get baptized." It wouldn't let me rest. I realize now it was the gentle leading of the Holy Spirit.

1. Prov 27:17.

For the Potential Christian

Finally, I couldn't take it anymore. The conviction was too strong. I decided that I must get baptized. I concluded that, if for no other reason, the fact that Jesus did it is good enough. After all, he is our example. There was no need for further argument at that point. So, I found a church, signed up, took the classes, and got baptized. It was literally a life-changing experience.

There are no words to describe the joy I felt before they dipped me into the baptismal pool. Or the peace I felt in my spirit as the water slowly rushed over my body. It was less than five seconds that I was under, but in that moment it felt like time had stopped. When I rose again, irrepressible tears were streaming from my eyes. My mind was far from the things of this world, and completely focused on God.

All I could do was cry tears of joy. I had finally done it. I had officially died and risen with Christ. I had been obedient, and it felt good. Afterward, a nice lady gave me a hug while the tears drained from my eyes. I was overwhelmed by God's love. I felt he was pleased with me that day, and if I could change anything about it, I'd do it sooner.

The bottom line is, if we are physically able, we should get baptized. I see no reason for Christians to be divided over this matter. It is commanded throughout Scripture, and when we truly become children of God, the Holy Spirit won't let us rest until we get it done. Furthermore, Jesus himself was baptized. We are in no way greater than Jesus, therefore, if it's good for him, then it's good for us. Baptism allows us to identify with Christ in his death, burial, and resurrection. It symbolizes the death of our old life and the birth of our new life, which we now live in obedience to God. It is truly an awesome experience.

But, understand that baptism should be done for the right reasons. It's not something we do just to say we did it; but it should only be done when we truly believe in the Gospel and have accepted Christ. Most churches have pre-baptism classes where you can learn more and ask questions. If you ever come to the fork in the road as to whether or not you should be baptized, my advice to you is this: don't waste time asking, "Why should I be baptized?"

So, What Now?

But, if you believe in the Son of God with all your heart, ask yourself, "Why shouldn't I?"[2]

The third tip is to read and study the Bible as often as possible. Never take anyone's word alone for what is in the Bible. Some teachings are not found anywhere in God's Word, but are made up by man, and some scriptures are often misquoted or misinterpreted. All of these are equally detrimental. When you hear someone speak about the things of God, their words should confirm what is in the Bible, adding nothing more and teaching nothing less. So, save yourself a world of confusion. Study the Bible and know it for yourself. This way you can avoid being a victim to false teachings and false teachers, which is very dangerous.

Okay, here's another tip. It's important to remember, because it's easy to forget in the heat of the moment. The enemy will try to come against you with everything he's got. He's going to tell you every lie possible to try and turn you away from God—especially in these new and fragile stages. He'll even use those closest to you to try and discourage you, but try not to be upset with them. Just know it's not them that speaks, but it's the spirit of the enemy using them and influencing their words and actions. Instead, pray for them. God can do more for our situation through prayer than we can do when we try to handle things ourselves.

Now, here's a good one to keep close. Satan will try to convince you that nothing about you has changed. He'll make you agree that you'll never be good enough, so that you'll give up and walk away from God. Remember he's the father of lies, so don't believe him. Whenever these thoughts begin to creep into your mind, resist them. Do not entertain them, not even for a moment. The longer you dwell on these thoughts, the more time you'll give the enemy to feed you more lies, and before you know it you'll start to believe them.

Instead, close your eyes, stand firm on the truth of God, and declare with authority, "Devil, you are a liar!" Then, go back to what you were doing. Don't give him an inch or else he'll take a mile. If you're not familiar with the Bible, search online for scriptures that

---

2. Acts 8:26–39 NKJV.

pertain to your situation and memorize them. When you sense a lie circling your mind, shoot it down before it lands by speaking the scriptures out loud.

One of the first passages I memorized as a new Christian was a verse I found online. It was a statement Jesus made to his disciples in Luke 10:19 and it reads, "Behold, I give you the authority to trample on serpents and scorpions, and over all the power of the enemy, and nothing shall by any means hurt you" (NKJV). I learned a portion of another passage, John 4:4, and what I took from that was this: "Greater is he that is in me than he who is in the world."

That was all the Scripture I knew at that point. But when I spoke these words with authority and refused to give in to sinful urges, *God* stepped in to defend me. As a father who gives his baby a boost when he sees them struggling to stand, my Father intervened and helped me to stand against sin and addiction. It was one of the hardest things I've ever done, but he gave me strength to resist what I could never resist on my own. The temptation would eventually leave, and as time went on it became easier to overcome. So, don't be fearful in the face of temptation. Stand up to it by standing on God's Word. Remember, through Jesus you have the power to make Satan flee![3]

Tip number six: don't get so caught up in the dos and the don'ts. We are saved by grace, through faith in Christ alone. We are not justified by anything we do—past, present, or future.[4] When I first became a Christian, I spent so much time worrying whether I should do this, or if I shouldn't do that. Don't do this to yourself as it will drive you crazy. However, that's not a green light to do what you please either. After all, we are representatives of God and must conduct ourselves as such. Instead, renew your mind by meditating daily on God's Word, and watch how it will change you.

Which brings me to my next point: in the Bible, many instructions are written in plain black and white. It's not a mystery, nor rocket science, but it's basically "thou shalt" or "thou shalt not." Still, some things are not as clear. Therefore, here's my advice: if

---

3. Jas 4:7.
4. Eph 2:8–9.

So, What Now?

it's plainly written in God's Word, follow it and do not question it. However, if it's not plainly written, seek wise counsel from brothers and sisters who have been walking a while in the faith, and pray for the Holy Spirit to help you understand.

Remember to always pray. In the morning, afternoon, during the day, before bed—pray. There will be times when you don't know what to say, but just begin to worship God and the Holy Spirit will lead you in prayer. Follow the leading of the Spirit, who will help you know what is right and what is wrong. He will change the desires of your heart to match what God desires for you, and gradually you'll see your life lining up with God's Word. I encourage you to dig deeper on your own to find out more about the Holy Spirit and how he empowers and helps every believer.

Here's something else to take note of: sometimes, when we change, we expect everyone around us to change also; but unfortunately it doesn't work like that—at least not right away. Take care that you don't look down on others who haven't made it to where you are yet. Always remember that if it weren't for the grace of God, their situation could be yours.

Be careful not to let your zeal for God turn into pride or arrogance. "God resists the proud, but gives grace to the humble."[5] Therefore, walk in a spirit of humility, and be open to receive godly advice and correction. Sometimes God will correct us directly, and other times he may use other believers to get a word of correction to us. It's not to make you feel bad, but it's to strengthen your relationship with Jesus.

Listen, we all make mistakes. Try not to get offended but receive the correction with grace, and pray about every message you're given. Just like earthly parents discipline their children, so does God discipline us. We all need correction from time to time. It doesn't feel good, but it's for our benefit. So, don't feel bad when it happens, but instead rejoice and be glad. Because God corrects the people he loves.[6]

---

5. 1 Peter 5:5 NKJV.
6. Hebrews 12:6.

For the Potential Christian

Finally, keep in mind that we're all growing in Christ. As we grow, we'll see magnificent changes taking place in our lives. Others around us, including those we're closest to, will notice these changes as well. It's a learning process. You won't know everything overnight, but you will have what you need each day.

At times you may get discouraged, but whatever you do, don't quit. Some days it won't be easy. Some weeks you won't know which road to take. But, if you're confused, uncertain, or overwhelmed about anything, stop and have a little talk with Jesus. It could be something as simple as, "God help me," and he will hear you. Rest assured he will work things out for you.

So, I say again, do *not* quit. God will never quit on you. Nobody can snatch you out of the Lord's hand,[7] therefore the only way you lose is if you give up and walk away from God. Lean on his strength. Reach for his wisdom. Press on and stay in the race. And if you do these things, and if you don't lose faith, you are guaranteed to win.

Walking consists of taking one step at a time. We can't click our heels and be where we need to be in the blink of an eye like Dorothy in The Wizard of Oz. Our Christian walk is a step-by-step journey, which means it's going to take time. However, the good news is, you've already taken that first step by accepting Christ. But there's a lot more area to cover. God has chosen you for a specific purpose, and your journey begins right now.

Along the way, I pray he will fight for you, strengthen you, and use you in an awesome and mighty way. Be encouraged! Don't lose heart! Stay as close as you can to Jesus. And if you stumble, don't give up. Get on your feet, dust yourself off, and allow God's grace to restore you. Whatever you do, don't sit down. Stand up straight, square your shoulders, put one foot in front of the other, and keep on stepping, my friend . . . keep on stepping.

Your sister in Christ,
Miranda

---

7. John 10:28–30.

So, What Now?

Trust in the Lord with all your heart,
And lean not on your own understanding;
In all your ways acknowledge Him,
And He shall direct your paths.[8]

---

8. Prov 3:5–6 NKJV.

Bibliography

Billy Graham Evangelistic Association. "Billy Graham's Answer: What Is Sin? Are All Sins Equal in God's Eyes?" March 26, 2014. https://billygraham.org/story/billy-grahams-answer-what-is-sin-are-all-sins-equal-in-gods-eyes/.

Billy Graham Evangelistic Association staff. "What Will Heaven Be Like?" June 1, 2004. https://billygraham.org/answer/what-will-heaven-be-like-2/.

Bryant, Al, ed. *Zondervan Compact Bible Dictionary*. Grand Rapids: Zondervan, 1994.

Duvall, J. Scott, and J. Daniel Hays. *Grasping God's Word: A Hands-On Approach to Reading, Interpreting, and Applying the Bible*. 3rd ed. Grand Rapids: Zondervan, 2012.

Graham, Billy. "Billy Graham: Things God Hates." *Decision Magazine*, February 19, 2020. https://decisionmagazine.com/things-god-hates/.

Holsteen, Nathan D., and Michael J. Svigel. *Exploring Christian Theology*. Vol. 2 of 3. Minneapolis: Bethany House, 2015.

Kohlenberger, John R., ed. *NIV Exhaustive Bible Concordance*. 3rd ed. Grand Rapids: Zondervan, 2015.

Prince, Derek. "Repentance." Sermon. Audio recording in two parts. Available at http://www.sermonindex.net/modules/mydownloads/viewcat.php?cid=206&min=20&orderby=titleA&show=20.

www.ingramcontent.com/pod-product-compliance
Lightning Source LLC
Chambersburg PA
CBHW070254100426
42743CB00011B/2243